Life After ...
Biological Sciences

Thousands of students graduate from university each year. The lucky few have the rest of their lives mapped out in perfect detail – but for most, things are not nearly so simple. Armed with your hard-earned degree, the possibilities and career paths lying before you are limitless, and the number of choices you suddenly have to make can seem bewildering.

Life After ... Biological Sciences has been written specifically to help students currently studying, or who have recently graduated, make informed choices about their future lives. It will be a source of invaluable advice and wisdom to graduates (whether you wish to use your degree directly or not), covering such topics as:

* Identifying a career path that interests you
* Seeking out an opportunity that matches your skills and aspirations
* Staying motivated and pursuing your goals
* Networking and self-promotion
* Making the transition from scholar to worker
* Putting the skills you developed at university to good use in life.

The *Life After ...* series of books are more than simple 'career guides'. They are unique in taking a holistic approach to career advice – recognising the increasing view that, although a successful working life is vitally important, other factors can be just as essential to happiness and fulfilment. They are *the* indispensible handbooks for students considering their future direction in life.

Sally Longson is a life coach and well-known writer and media commentator in the field of careers.

Also available from Sally Longson

Life After ... Business and Administrative Studies
978-0-415-37591-7

Life After ... Engineering and Built Environment
978-0-415-37592-4

Life After ... Language and Literature
978-0-415-37593-1

Life After ... Art and Design
978-0-415-37590-0

Life After ... Social Studies
978-0-415-41247-6

Life After ... Biological Sciences
978-0-415-41249-0

Life After ...
Biological Sciences

A practical guide to life after your degree

Sally Longson

Taylor & Francis Group

LONDON AND NEW YORK

First published 2007
by Routledge
2 Park Square, Milton Park, Abingdon, Oxon OX14 4RN

Simultaneously published in the USA and Canada
by Routledge
270 Madison Ave, New York, NY 10016

Routledge is an imprint of the Taylor & Francis Group, an informa business

© 2007 Sally Longson

Typeset in Sabon by
HWA Text and Data Management, Tunbridge Wells
Printed and bound in Great Britain by
MPG Boooks Ltd, Bodmin

British Library Cataloguing in Publication Data
A catalogue record for this book is available from the British Library

Library of Congress Cataloging-in-Publication Data
Longson, Sally
  Life after – art and design: a practical guide to life after your degree/
  Sally Longson. – 1st ed.
    p.   cm.
  Includes bibliographical references and index.
  1. Art – Vocational guidance. 2. College graduates – Vocational
  guidance.
  I. Title: Practical guide to life after your degree. II. Title
  N8350.L66 2006
  702.3´73–dc22   2005036629

ISBN10: 0–415–41249–8 (pbk)
ISBN10: 0–203–94056–3 (ebk)

ISBN13: 978–0–415–41249–0 (pbk)
ISBN13: 978–0–203–94056–3 (ebk)

Contents

Preface

Your degree over – or nearly over – you contemplate your next move, rather like a game of chess. You plot your next move, you fall into it, or someone makes you fall into it. Life is continually like a game of chess, but checkmate – the end result – is entirely where you or someone else decides it is to be. You can plan to move forward and make progress, or you can feel like a pawn, moved around a board at someone else's bidding.

As you read this page, look out across the blue sea and skies before you and cast your mind and eyes to the opportunities beyond them. Life lies before you like a huge ocean. The question is, where are you headed next? Who and what do you want on board? Where will your future port be?

Opportunities abound for the biological sciences graduate in a world full of discovery and the quest for knowledge and its application to business, life, communities, the planet, people and animals. You could be working on a research project which takes you to meetings and conferences in Stockholm, San Francisco and Shanghai, working with like-minded people, comparing notes, exchanging ideas, sharing frustrations, hopes and excitement. Collaboration, team work, autonomy, responsibility, the search for answers ... the scientist has an exciting career ahead indeed. The knowledge economy in many countries is growing, with clusters of companies, spin-offs, national health authorities such as the National Health Service (NHS) in the UK, local government, research institutes, government agencies, health organisations, the water, agricultural and environmental industries, conservation charities, and more, all looking to recruit biological science graduates who can work well in a team, meet deadlines, communicate to those who have no knowledge or understanding of science, and use the skills they have to discover, research, amaze and track down answers.

The stock of biological science students, certainly in the UK, is projected to increase by 76.7 per cent between 2004 to 2014, according to the Department of Trade and Industry's report of March 2006, *Science, Engineering and Technology Skills in the UK.* The Sector Skills Development Agency report *Working Futures 2004–2014* projects that there will be an 18 per cent increase in science and technology professionals, and a 30 per cent increase for associate professionals. The increased demand for science and technology professionals in the UK will, in part, be due to expansion but also to replace those staff who are retiring or leaving the profession for other reasons. And of course, the science, engineering and technology sectors need young people to come through, excited and enlivened by what they have been taught at school, college and university, and also by the way they have been taught. Teachers, tutors and lecturers play a key role in producing the scientists of tomorrow, and therein lies opportunity for the person who can inspire, excite, enthuse and lead others. Our world needs you to help bring on the future scientists, mathematicians, engineers and technologists of tomorrow. The profession also needs those strong in communication so that the rest of us can understand the implications of research, discovery and development, and deal with them accordingly.

Of course, many biological science graduates choose to move on and do something else, rather than remain in academia and/or research. Many enter professional services where their knowledge of science will be invaluable to a future employer and will complement their work nicely. Elsewhere, if you choose to leave your scientific knowledge behind and move to fresh fields, your drive to be meticulous, thorough and accurate, and to question and resolve will be appreciated by many employers.

Having a degree does not guarantee having a good job. *Nothing* in life guarantees you a job. You may experience stints of lower level work in retail, leisure and tourism, and administration, as sales assistants, waiters and administrators, and find yourself wondering what university was for. The key to success is to keep your head, and put your career and life desires firmly at the forefront of your mind, focus and efforts. There is expected to be a significant increase in the numbers of managers, professional occupations, association professional and technical occupations, and personal service occupations, especially in teaching, research and science, business and public service. Those who persist in striving for a career and a life will succeed in their efforts; those who give up will have a lesser quality life than they could have and deserve.

You may land yourself a job, but if you want a *great* job you need to put in persistent effort to think long term and not just to pay day, and to give back and contribute rather than take. Like any relationship in life, a career needs nurturing.

Whatever stage you have reached, you are at a great time to assess your life and what you want out of it. Use the exercises in this book to help you determine just that. A career is only part of life – there are a whole host of other things which are important too, such as relationships, finance and lifestyle. The main emphasis of this book will be on career and work, but you can transfer many of the tips and advice regarding those on to other segments of life.

While you were at university, you chose to head straight out of those zones you normally felt comfortable in. You tested yourself in every aspect of life, and enjoyed it. It is time to leave that comfort zone again and take risks to move on and make the most of your life ahead. Let's get started.

Chapter 1

Decisions, decisions ...

What happens now? What happens next?

What happens from now in your life depends on how determined you are to turn your hopes, aspirations, dreams and ambitions into being, and what sort of journeys, adventures, fun and experience you want to enjoy in it. Your future plans may already be known to you; you may be kicking lots of ideas about, or just not have a clue. What you *do* know is that there are lots of decisions to make, plans to be laid and things to do – but what, exactly? Where do you start?

Looking at the next few months

If you've already left university, you may happily spend the summer having a break at home before considering what happens next. The start of the academic year may feel strange as you realise that for the first time, perhaps in your life, you don't have to go back to a new term. You can do as you like. This may also be strange to the people you live with, such as your parents. They may not be used to you being around and may start giving you odd jobs to do which interfere with your day and which you may resent. Meal times may be punctuated with discussions about your future and when you're going to get a 'real' job; visitors to the house ask whether you've got a job yet. It may feel as if life is going backwards or standing still, instead of moving forward. Build a routine into your life, even if you have no work or study to go to. It will help you when you start work.

You may have studied part time for your degree while holding down a full-time job, working two or three hours a night and trying the patience of loved ones as you disappear to study yet again. You've probably pleaded with the boss for more time off, spent lunch times doing research on the internet and sneaked the odd sickie to get that assignment done. And now you're faced with many free hours and you feel a bit lost. It's nice to have a rest from all that study, but having risen to one challenge, you want another.

Whether you are an undergraduate or a postgraduate, if you're still at university, create time now in your week to plan your career. Think ahead. Participate in activities such as constructive work experience, internships, develop your web of industry contacts, voluntary work, attend careers and trade events, research the job market, find out what resources are available if you want to become self-employed, consider further study, visit the careers service in person and online, and analyse your own strengths and capabilities. Fill any gaps in your skills base which may show up on your CV. Do something unusual which really will make you stand out from other candidates. Employers are often looking for that one line which makes them sit up and think, *Wow, I've got to meet this person!*

Start building bridges from where you are now and where you want to be. The more foundations you can lay down now, the easier life will be later.

Take control. Get organised

Create a folder – call it something like 'Life After University' – and put everything in it you need to work on to save yourself time rummaging for information here and there. Create a career folder on your PC or laptop for email. Bookmark useful websites you refer to continually. Efficient organisation will clear your mind of clutter and enable you to think more clearly. Your 'life after' folder should grow week by week as you add to it and expand your knowledge, contacts, ideas and work.

Then look ahead

There are several decisions to make about your life after graduating. These vary from the urgent and/or important, to those things which simply need to be dealt with, such as *'What will I do with all my books and materials?'* and *'Which friends do I want to keep in touch with?'*. There will be urgent decisions you need to make today. The important ones are not usually time pressured but they affect the big picture, i.e. your life. An important and urgent decision may be: Do you accept that offer of a postgraduate place you had yesterday? It's Tuesday now, you have until Thursday at 5 p.m. to decide.

Two major issues you'll need to deal with are those of career and finance. Devote more time and energy to these now. Socialising may be fun but it won't bring you the best rate of return career-wise, nor will it help you pay off your debts. Plotting your career and working up the ladder will bring a higher salary, and you'll need to apply discipline and rigour to managing your finances if you are to clear your debts. Let's follow these two areas in life further.

Do career and financial audits

Table 1.1 demonstrates questions to ponder.

Doing an audit like this empowers you because you're choosing to address your situation, dealing with known facts rather than assumptions or guesses, so it's easier to move forward and take action. With regard to debts, it is better to know what your bottom

Table 1.1

Career	Finance
What do I want to achieve in life?	How much do I owe?
What is important to me?	Who do I owe it to?
What do I have to offer the world?	How much interest am I paying each lender monthly?
What am I going to do next?	
What could I learn to ensure I get to where I want to be?	What could I do to reduce this interest?
What are my ambitions and aspirations, dreams and hopes?	What incomings do I have now?
How far do I want a career which uses my degree knowledge?	What am I spending it on?
	What do I have left?
Could I go on to further study?	What could I do to cut back on my spending?
Do I need a break?	
Where in the world do I want to work?	How could I pay back my loans and debts?
How far shall I go in my career?	Who could help me?
Where can I get constructive, informed advice, e.g. university careers service, Prospects?	What could I do to get the best deal on everything?
	What could I do to supplement my income?
Where can I go for help with this sector?	When will I start paying everything back?
Who can I approach?	Where can I get constructive, informed advice, e.g. bank, building society, student loan company?
Who do I need to support me?	
What action(s) will I take to move me closer to where I want to be?	What action(s) will I take?

line is to prevent getting further into debt. You may have a student debt of £15,000, but how much further are you prepared to allow it to increase before you start paying it back? £20,000? £30,000? It doesn't mean you'll never go out for a wild night out with your friends again; you could all look for other ways to have a wild time which controls the finances more firmly. Yes, there are times when we don't like the decisions we have to make; they are uncomfortable and don't fit in well with the lifestyle we want. But discipline never did anyone any harm and can frequently bring unexpected rewards, not least of which is self-respect and an in-built self-belief that you can turn an uncomfortable situation around.

Take action now!

1 List the decisions you need to make now and in the next six months. Which ones need to be dealt with first?
2 What have you done so far towards making these decisions?
3 What else do you need to do or to know to decide? How will you get that information and where will you get it from?
4 Whose help will you need?
5 When do you need to make each decision?
6 What action will you take?

Many of the decisions in one area of our life will impact on others. For instance, your career choice will affect where you live and work, the structure of your life and the people you work with and/or socialise with. It will impact on your standard of living and your overall happiness, the hours you work and whether you're on call or not, the pace of your working day and your stress levels. You may need to undertake further training, learning and development to acquire your professional status. The effort you put into your career will affect your ability to pay back your loans and start laying strong financial foundations to your life.

Are you an effective decision maker?

You can learn a lot about yourself from the way you've made past decisions in all areas of your life, from course choice, relationships and health, to the way you spend your leisure time. Take two decisions you've made about your university life or course. Ask yourself:

1   What motivated you to take these decisions?
2   *How* did you make them – gut instinct, careful research and thought, weighing up the pros and cons, tossing a coin, following the lead of others, force of circumstance or meeting the expectations of others? What process do you follow?
3   Who influenced your decisions and subsequent actions? Who could you have involved more or less?
4   What, if anything, held you back from making decisions and how did you overcome it?
5   Is a pattern emerging about your decision making? What does it tell you about the way you make decisions? Are there patterns which aren't helping you that you need to break?
6   How can you make your decision making more effective in your career and life overall?

In making any decision, there are various factors to take into account as Table 1.2 shows.

Table 1.2

Possible factors influencing your decision	Choosing modules to study	Choosing your career
Your strengths and skills	What you're naturally good at and wanted to build your skills in	Same for career
Your interests	Following your passions	Same for career – this is what you want to do
What was available?	The modules on offer at your university	What is on offer in the region you work in?
Personal fit	You had a lot of time and respect for the tutor and thought he'd bring out the best in you	You like where the company is going and what it stands for; you met the guys and felt comfortable with them
Long-term plans	You want to go into self-employment so this fitted well with your career plans	You choose an employer who can meet your aspirations
How you make decisions	*for example ...* 'Ran out of time – just ticked the box for something to do' 'Gut feeling. Everything felt right about this'	*for example ...* 'Went for the first thing I saw – can always change later' 'The moment I walked into the place, I knew it was right for me'

Decision-making skills transfer well in life, from making career choices to buying a home. They are essential at work, whether you are self-employed, an employee, or the boss. Tenacity is vital too: action plans to implement our decisions are often interrupted by (unexpected) obstacles, making the journey en route more of a roller-coaster of a ride, but a focus on the end result will help you to steer through the rougher patches.

Focus on the result you want and the obstacles will shrink

Often when faced with a decision, we tend to focus too much on potential problems. *'There are too many graduates ...'*, *'not enough time in the day ...'*, *'I don't want to ...'*. Problems have a way of shrinking when put into the context of what we really want. Let's say you are offered a dream career from an employer you'd love to work for but you don't know anyone in the town you'd be living in. *'Where will I live if I go somewhere new?'* you may ask. But compared to the job offer, which you're wild with excitement over, the accommodation problem is minor. You know you'll sort it out somehow. The most important thing is that you have the offer you wanted. You found somewhere to live at university; you can do it again.

Have faith in your own ability to create a life for yourself even if you move to a place where you know no one.

It isn't easy, but you've done it before and survived – and you've developed strong transferable skills at university, such as the abilities to:

1   Start completely afresh – new people, new place, new things to learn, new challenges.
2   Take part in and contribute to an organisation – previously, your university, now the workplace, the community, new friends.
3   Find your way around and learn the ropes.
4   Ask the right questions of the right people to get the answers you need.
5   Network and get to know people across the organisation – as you did at university.

6   Take the initiative and make things happen in a day at university or college which – lectures and tutorials apart – is pretty much your own.
7   Show how adaptable and flexible you are at juggling work, study and social activities, often changing plans at the last minute.
8   Organise your time.
9   Hunt out new friends and like-minded people you can particularly relate to.
10   Relate to people of different sorts of backgrounds, nationalities and abilities.

You'll need every single one of these skills at work, though probably using them with more formality than you would at university. Your academic experience has taught you to think, to question, to be creative, to think laterally, to challenge, to research, to find problems to solutions and to interact. Those skills will never be wasted. And the more you stretch yourself and expand them, the more powerful a resource they will become.

Wait a minute ...

Before you start making decisions, consider what's really important to you.

Where are you going? How does the decision fit into the bigger picture?

A key starting point to making successful decisions involves knowing what is right for you in life or work. You need a strong sense of self-worth and self-awareness. These things encompass areas such as the roles you want to play in life, your career interests, ambitions, aspirations, the environments and conditions you thrive in and learn best in, the things you need around you to make you happy and feel fulfilled and those things that are important to you and what you couldn't do without, i.e. your values. Know what you want, and life has more purpose. It goes deeper than this: you need to consider your purpose in being here on earth; why you have the skills, talents and capabilities and personality that you do, and how you can best contribute them to a rapidly changing world.

Know yourself and what you want and you'll move faster to get it – you're less likely to deviate and waste time. Many people simply wait for that lucky break to knock on their door. Unfortunately, they have a long wait. You can create your own luck, as Dr Wiseman points out in his excellent book *The Luck Factor* (see Further Reading).

What's important to you?

When you live by your values, you look forward to the start of a new day or week, and you wake up with a happy heart. Life feels right: you feel fulfilled with a strong sense of your own self-worth. Your goals, hopes and aspirations seem easier to work for because you're at your best as you strive towards them. You know you're making the right choices and decisions and moving in the right direction. Similarly, the company which recruits staff with values equal to its own has a good feel about it. The staff are happy, motivated, fulfilled and feel appreciated. They look forward to going to work and are a tight-knit team.

Five signs when life – and work in particular – does not encapsulate your values

1   You're exhausted trying to work at something that doesn't gel with you while pretending that all is well.
2   You're frustrated and short tempered, especially as Monday looms.
3   It's lonely. Everyone else seems to be on a different wavelength to you.
4   You keep thinking, *There must be more to life than this!* This thought persists over time, making you increasingly frustrated and angrier.
5   You're disappointed in yourself because you know that you should cut your losses and leave, but you can't find the *courage* to do it.

Of course, you may find the perfect match and then something hinders its progression: a technological innovation, a change in the markets, a drop in demand, restructuring, redundancy. Employers understand that it takes time to find the right match, and when reading your CV, they consider your achievements, progression, development, future career plans and the person who lies behind the words on paper and portfolio. But it's your responsibility to find the career and role you want. You need to be prepared to move to find the right next move even if this means going through the rigmarole of job hunting or hooking the right contract every two or three years.

Table 1.3 gives examples of life and career values. Which ones are important to you to have or be in your life and career to make you truly happy and feel successful?

Having considered which values are important to you, you can build a life and career which incorporates them. For example, if achievement is very important to you, you could look for careers where results are exceedingly important and measured, such as sales roles.

Choose the top eight values which are essential to you from those you've ticked above and create a picture of what they mean to you – don't make any assumptions about them. Get the foundations right. If you think that things such as travel, holidays and a good social life are your values, consider what those things *give you* or *provide you with* and you'll have your real values. Then rank your eight values in order. Which one is the most important? Which values could you *not* do without? And which are you *not* prepared to compromise on? Now that you have your list of values in life, you

Table 1.3

Winner	Participant	Contributor
Continuous change	Change where needed	Little change
Security	Stability	Risk
Creativity	Performer	Conformity
Compassion	Fair	Faith
Achiever	Influencer	Supporter
Recognition	Status in community	Appreciated
Success	Work–life balance	Fulfilment
Autonomy	Independence	Managed
Visionary	Implement	Support
Adventure	Spirituality	Pleasure
Driver, creator	Follow the leader	Win–win
Wealth	Rewarded	Feel-good factor
Happiness	Freedom	Discoverer
Other	Other	Other

can benchmark decisions and plans against them to ensure that the things you want are in line with them.

Compromising in life will bring more win–wins

At some stage in life, you'll need to compromise. For example, let's say you want to work for an ethical company, but the only position you were offered was from a company which was unethical in your eyes. What would you do? Would you refuse to take the job and uphold your values or accept the offer and move on as soon as you could?

So what happens now?

Figure 1.1 gives you questions to ponder and answer.

| Now, today | What do you want to happen between these events? When do you want them to take place? | Next 3–5 years |

- Find and complete a PhD in ...
- Manage a team in a lab of researchers
- Have professional qualifications in accountancy and a job in the pharmaceuticals sector
- Get qualified as ... with a view to setting up my own business
- Work in China as ...
- Qualified as a ...
- Paid off ...% of my student loans and started to ...
- Found my partner for life

Figure 1.1

Many graduates have no clear idea of what they want to do after university, so they take whatever comes their way in the first three to five years after graduation, as Figure 1.2 shows.

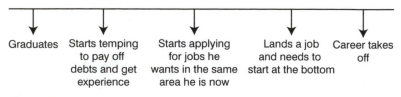

| Graduates | Starts temping to pay off debts and get experience | Starts applying for jobs he wants in the same area he is now | Lands a job and needs to start at the bottom | Career takes off |

Figure 1.2

This runway to career take-off may be longer and tougher in terms of getting that lucky break, the opportunity or gap in the market, especially as you are probably trying to begin a new life at the same time. You may hook a lower-level job to get going; if that's you, keep a focused eye on your future and exhort persistent effort in working towards it. Take your eye off that future, and you'll lose your focus; your ambitions will take longer to achieve, or they may lose their impetus and fizzle out.

Do you want a job, a career or a business?

These are very different things. Jobs fit well into short-term plans and bring the money in, but they don't necessarily stretch you or pay well. Consequently, they can make you feel bored and disillusioned, especially when you weigh up your salary against your student debts. Careers run over a course of time, enabling you to develop your skills, expertise and experience in one particular sector, often climbing a ladder to reach the upper echelons of the business and sector or academic environment. You may have a view of the top of this ladder from the bottom or you may create the view rung by rung as you climb up. Of course, a job can become a career if you take the initiative, yank it up a gear and get yourself noticed. You could set up your own business, which enables *you* to make all the decisions: what you will sell, the who, what, when, why, how and where.

How does your career fit into your life?

You need to find the work–life balance that's right for you, your life and your dependents. At first, this may be hindered as you devote time to establishing yourself and get a foot on the work and housing ladders, putting bricks and blocks down to get the life you want – the house, family life, network of friends, security, professional qualifications where appropriate, the opportunity for advancement and professional growth, recognition and appreciation. You may prefer to focus on having fun, rather than sorting your career and life out. *Well, there's always next year.*

A hunger for success at work, a discovery or the search for an answer to a particular question can seriously impact on our quality of life. If, as a scientist, you were so determined to find the answers you were looking for that you worked 14-hour days Monday to

Fridays, 11 hours on a Saturday and then some more on a Sunday, how would you also handle time for family, relationships, your own wellbeing and the daily administration that keeps life running smoothly? You may be prepared to give that earlier in your career if it takes you to where you really want to be, or you may prefer to opt for a more sensible work–life balance which takes you to a rung on the ladder which you're happy with.

What matters is the *degree of control* we each have over our work–life balance. If you decide to work 100 hours a week to make that first million, that's your choice. Work–life balance becomes an issue when we feel we *don't* have a choice; that other people are making decisions for us about the hours we need to put in. Some employers place a higher priority on work–life balance than others. The *New Scientist Careers Guide 2007* shows that more scientists wanted overtime as a perk, which should be telling you something about the hours they are putting in – yet they are not alone. Note that we can elect to work long hours for the wrong reasons – work can provide that perfect escape from other areas which aren't going so well: unhappy relationships at home, a lack of social life, not knowing how to meet people in the right area. If you're working long hours, ask yourself why, and what's really driving you to do it.

As you create a vision of your future career, ask yourself questions such as:

- What is your career goal, outcome or end result? If it makes things easier, look at this over a three to five year period.
- Why is this important to you?
- How exactly is your career important to you?
- Where do you want to be doing it?
- When are your timescales/deadlines for achieving your goal?
- Who will you be doing it with?
- Who can help you?
- How will you get there? What are the different ways you could reach the outcome you want?
- What can you do to boost your chances of success?
- What can you control? What is outside your control?
- Which deadlines do you need to look out for, such as applying for postgraduate courses, work experience placements and internships?

♦ What in life and in your career are you *not* prepared to risk, such as your integrity, values, standards, expectations of yourself, key relationships, and what *are* you prepared to risk.

The *why* is important. If you don't understand *why* something is important to you, it is far less likely to happen. If you understand what is important to you about a decision – for example, keeping fit is important to you because you value good health which gives you the freedom to live your life to the full – then you're more likely to achieve it.

Wherever you are, pinpoint careers help available to you

Find out what careers advisory services are available to you where you are *now*, face to face, online and by telephone. Sometimes you just need to sit down and talk through your future with someone you can trust who is impartial, qualified and trained. Tap into local universities and colleges, your old university and other private agencies in your area for access to careers information and support. Most higher education institutions allow graduates to use their facilities for up to two or three years after graduation and they may also help graduates from any university wishing to move into, remain in or return to their area. (You may be charged for some services.)

Use the forward and strategic planning skills you acquired during your university life to plan your career and life.

Summary action points

Look back at your life overall:

1   How much has it consisted of what you want so far? What efforts have you put in to make sure that happened?
2   What clues do your past choices give you as you look into your future?
3   What do you want to achieve *in your life* in the next five years? What would that mean to you?

Chapter 2

Creating your career

This chapter is all about helping you create a vision of what you want your career to consist of. Even if you have an idea, use the self-assessment exercises to add depth to it or confirm that your idea is heading in the right direction. As a biological sciences graduate, you have a considerable variety of choices before you: many employers don't require graduates with a particular subject, but do have a preference for those with technical and/or numerical skills and knowledge.

Rather than canter laboriously through one career after another, this chapter will pose various questions for you to ask yourself when plotting your career, so that you can highlight what is important to you.

What are your passions and motivations?

If you want to be happy and successful in your career, get passionate. Find something to do which really inspires and motivates you, and stirs you to action. Consider the following questions:

+ What excites and inspires you? What grabs your interest over a sustained period of time?
+ What are you passionate about?
+ What do you want to make a difference to or particularly do something about?
+ How do you want to make a difference to the world, a local community or a group of people?
+ What problem do you most want to solve?
+ What secret dreams and aspirations do you have? How could your degree and life experiences so far help you to fulfil them?

- What makes you jump out of bed in the morning? What could you work all day at and then plough into the night over?
- What drives your passions and lies behind them? What does your passion give you that nothing else does?
- What do you most look forward to?

What do you want to contribute to the world?

Have you thought about the contribution you can make to society, your local community, customers, clients and people? Take time to answer these questions:

1 What role do you want to play in changing our world? Do you want to change the way we think about it, or the knowledge we have?
2 What impact do you want your skills and talents and capabilities to have on the world around you?
3 What do you most want to make a difference to? Do you want this to happen in your capacity as a scientist?
4 Is there anything you feel particularly strongly about happening in the world that you want to change?
5 Who do you most want to help or work for?
6 What do you most want to contribute to humanity and the animal kingdom?
7 What sort of sector do you want to be surrounded by and work in?
8 What particular sectors and industries do you want to be closely allied to and work with?
9 What do you see as your most important purpose being at work and on this planet?
10 How could your degree help you achieve your answers above?

The answer to the last question will help you ascertain how big a part in your future biological sciences will play.

How relevant do you want your career to be to your degree?

Your answer to the above question will impact on your career choice and the opportunities ahead. For example, to move towards making your answers to the questions above happen, do you want to:

* Use your degree knowledge and expand it.
* Use your degree skills to complement your main role – your science knowledge is useful at work and relevant to the sector you're working in, but you deal with other aspects of the company.
* Do something completely different.

Let's consider these in turn.

Take up a career directly related to your degree

There are a number of careers directly relating to biological sciences where your scientific knowledge is placed squarely at the centre of your daily work, such as:

* Research and development in an area of which you have specialist expertise, working for universities, private companies or research institutes; opportunities abound also in the health service. *New Scientist* jobs (www.newscientist.com/jobs) has about 45 disciplines in biology on its job search pages, with a choice of the academic, government and industry sectors.
* Communicating: being a science or a technical writer, developing health campaigns. Can you take a subject of which you may have a very thorough grounding in technical terms and write about it in such terms as a lay person can understand, or for a scientific audience? There are other options here, such as working in public relations for a scientific company.
* Educating: teaching people of any age, most specifically young people in schools, colleges and universities, but also outside the education sector in its most formal context, i.e. visiting schools, giving talks to the public, leading walks and producing educational resources.
* Environmental conservation and management, working in research, advisory work, perhaps for wildlife trusts, conservation agencies, and government bodies.

The career you choose now can impact on your future working life; for example, research and development may see you moving into quality control, regulatory work, business development or leading a team of researchers. To get a feel for how this may look, build up a picture of any sector or niche area which appeals. Brainstorm – perhaps with your peers – to grasp the full extent of the opportunities before you, to acquire a full idea of where you can apply for jobs and where your skills, knowledge and expertise could be found wanting. Figure 2.1 gives examples of where you could be involved in educating – and this is by no means an exhaustive number.

Within each speciality that contributes to the overall field of biological sciences, some employers will inevitably be looking for a greater specialist knowledge of a subject than others so you may need to take a postgraduate qualification. Taking such a step can certainly influence the level at which you enter your chosen field. Delve further to find out what openings are available to you with your particular subject. There are websites worldwide to help you

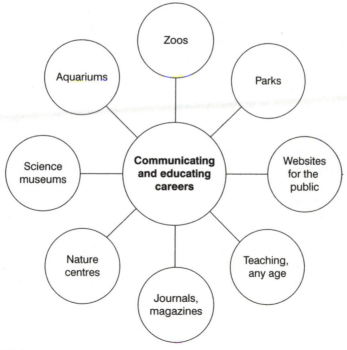

Figure 2.1

in the decision-making process; some are listed at the end of this chapter, yet more in Useful Addresses and Further Information.

Looking at research

You may decide to pursue a career in research or lecturing. According to Higher Education Statistics Agency Staff Records, there was a 26 per cent increase in the number of permanent academic staff in biological sciences between 1995 and 2003. Postgraduate students are building up a very high level of knowledge, understanding and expertise in a particular field. A postgraduate course will be essential if you want to move into areas such as academic research.

The Research Assessment Exercise means that the higher education funding bodies can distribute funds for research on quality. Find out more by visiting www.rae.ac.uk for information on the Research Assessment Exercise 2008; and www.hero.ac.uk/rae for 2001's results. Ratings give an idea of the standard of UK research. See Further Reading for more useful addresses.

One question you will need to ask yourself is *where* you wish to research. In academic life, you'll feel pressure to publish and produce articles – your university will want to make a good showing in the Research Assessment Exercises. You could also find yourself on a number of committees, teaching students and helping out your supervisor in more ways than you imagine. Industry will put the pressure on to ensure that you meet your clients' deadlines, to take patents out for new discoveries, to consider the bottom line for the company over all and you'll also need business awareness. The question is, if you wish to work on something you're passionate about and want to find out more about, do you wish to follow your own project (as you would in academic life or a research institute) or are you happy to work on someone else's quest for answers, such as a client in industry? Researchers are often also employed by research councils, the government and other relevant organisations to fulfil various responsibilities such as management, policy advice and project planning. In addition, higher education institutions often hire research staff to work on a contract basis to help with a particular piece of research. The website www.hero.ac.uk has more information on contract research.

Use your science skills to complement your main role

According to the Higher Education Statistics Agency's *Destination of Leavers Survey, 2003–2004*, 79 per cent of biological science students choose to enter an occupation which was outside science, technology, engineering and mathematics (STEM). This does not include those who go into teaching. And based on a Labour Force Survey (Autumn 2004) and the paper *Science, Engineering and Technology Skills in the UK* written by the DTI in March 2006, just 46 per cent of graduates in these categories enter STEM professions.

As the science sector grows and develops, private companies will require the support of many professionals from finance, human resources (HR), information technology (IT), marketing and public relations. Enter the opportunities for the biological science graduate with a thorough grounding in science, and its ways of working, but an ability to relate information and facts into terms non-scientists can understand and grasp. An HR manager with a science background will be far more helpful to the biotech company than the HR manager with a degree in, say, English literature. He knows what science is about, understands the sector and research and empathises with the quest for answers and knowledge. But he'll also have a business hat on. In cases such as these, advertisements for posts may stress something like 'first degree in biological sciences preferred' and if that is the case, provided you send in a carefully written application, you know you'll have an advantage over other applicants.

Other examples of these roles are:

* advisory work for organisations and companies in the science, health or medicine sectors;
* sales and/or marketing in industry and commerce, healthcare and medicine where a knowledge and understanding of science boosts your effectiveness;
* management in industrial companies, the NHS, government agencies;
* investor relations, liaising with those individuals and companies who control the funding;
* public relations – being the face of the company and projecting the right company image to a non-science specialist public;
* consultancy services, looking at areas such as IT, HR, logistics, processes and suggesting improvements;

- business development to ensure company growth, while understanding the pressures scientists work under;
- dealing with business finance: venture capitalists and undertaking equity research, while understanding the highs and lows of the path to discovery;
- accountancy, working as a finance director perhaps for a pharmaceutical company once you're qualified, where your understanding of the process of discovery can add to your business acumen and overall powers;
- investment banking, advising companies on how best to raise money to undergo major changes, perhaps done by a merger with or take-over of another company;
- protecting and commercialising ideas and projects resulting from research.

The level of knowledge you will need and use will depend on the role you are seeking; your scientific knowledge and background could benefit you in areas such as journalism, publishing, financial services, management, the Civil Service and the professions such as accountancy and law.

Changing track altogether

It could be that you've decided its time to part company with science and move to something new. Graduates have a wider choice of careers than ever before: management, administrative posts in the public and private sector and IT, management accountancy, sales and marketing, and buying and purchasing all need graduates and many have graduate trainee schemes. There are also back office support roles in operations and compliance, administration and office management. Executive assistants and personal assistants are increasingly taking on the work of junior and middle management.

Many graduates move into lower level work for which a degree is not required, such as retail, bar and restaurant work, and lower level administrative roles, often just to get the money coming in. If you take this track, you will need to dig deeper to yank yourself out if you want to change career or progress, and you won't enjoy the same salaries and perks those higher up the career ladder are starting to enjoy. Dissatisfaction may rise to give thoughts such as *'Why did I go to university and land myself with such a debt?'*. Plot and plan your way out of it.

Transferable skills are common to every career. Use them to sell yourself into new areas of work and career.

However relevant your work is to your degree, you'll need key transferable skills to succeed at work, such as:

1 Time management: identifying your priorities, meeting deadlines, giving time to what is important (such as business development activities).

2 Business development: pitching for and winning business and contracts; negotiating skills; building client relationships; obtaining feedback on your services and how they can be improved and enhanced; networking; creating a vision and deciding how to implement it.

3 Commercial awareness; an understanding of how business works (and an ability to speak the corporate language and that of your chosen sector).

4 Self-promotion skills and the ability to inspire confidence.

5 Communication skills, cultural awareness, tact, diplomacy and firmness.

6 Showing initiative and fresh thinking, a tenacity to seek new solutions to old problems.

7 The ability to drive your own continued career development: technical expertise, business know-how, IT knowledge where appropriate, changes and trends in the workplace.

8 For the self-employed wannabes: administration, bookkeeping, budgeting, business development, sales, marketing, advertising and public relations skills, networking and negotiating. Of course, you could outsource some of these tasks.

What role do you want to have?

Within any organisation, you'll have different levels of careers, attained as people work their way up the ladder. The role you aspire to will need its own strategy for development, for example, if you're looking to take on more of a business development role and have your own company one day, then business experience and, who knows, perhaps an MBA may be for you. The role you want will also depend on your values. If you're a risk taker, then you may be quite happy with contract work, not knowing what will happen at the end of each stint. If you're a natural leader, you may be happy to take the managing director position later on in your career. In considering this, you can look for companies which will help you to fulfil your aspirations, maybe not in six months after graduating, but over the forthcoming ten years, depending on how far you want to go. Do you want to be, for example:

- A company owner –
  Smaller micro-business owner.
- A leader –
  The boss, team leader, managing director, CEO, chairman.
- A manager –
  Project manager, in charge of a team of researchers.
  Finance manager, in charge of the budget.
- A technician –
  Lab technician.
- A support person, ensuring everything runs smoothly behind the scenes –
  Facilities manager, building manager, executive assistant.
- An entrepreneur –
  Patenting an idea and turning it into a product.
- A researcher –
  Working to produce new products and services, to innovate.

Look back at any relevant work experience you've had relating to the career you want. Think carefully back to everyone you met at the company or organisation. Make a note of all their roles. Some may have been scientific, such as the drug developer or medical specialist; others may have involved sales, marketing, HR, IT or finance matters where scientific knowledge wasn't so important. Consider which role might suit you best. Look, too, at your involvement in extra-curricular activities – what is your preferred role, and why?

The pros of moving up the career ladder include better pay and perks, being able to contribute to the company's direction, and helping your team grow and progress. There are cons, too: management responsibilities may take you away from the work you really want to do, and they will almost certainly follow you home. The boss may spend a lot of time in client meetings, looking at profit and loss figures, dealing with HR issues, thinking about the future and more. The ability to communicate and empathise becomes even more important as you progress. You may need to move companies every two or three years to acquire the progression you want.

What results do you want to achieve?

You can get a certain idea for where your future lies by considering the results you want to achieve at work.

Looking back over your degree studies and life experience to date:

- What were the three most important achievements you have had?
- What did they have in common?
- What results were involved in them?
- How do those results relate to the world of work?
- What results would you like your efforts at work to have most of all?
- Who would you like them to affect most?

Examples of results are:

- making a discovery
- expanding knowledge
- expanding knowledge and creating a commercial produce as a result
- clinching the deal or sale
- influencing a group or an individual or the direction something takes
- creating a new policy, procedure or regulation
- turning an idea into a product or service
- recognition
- justice
- making customers happy
- making progress in an experiment
- making huge profits
- making a difference to a cause, a person, a community, a group, an animal, nature
- a change in circumstances
- a merger, take-over
- financing something or someone and seeing an end result
- an award
- information needed by a client.

How hungry are you to make these achievements happen?

Look at the results you've highlighted. How hungry are you for them? Are you ravenous to make them happen or just happy to nibble at them? How fulfilled would you be if you were hungry and driven enough to achieve the results you wanted every working day, 48 weeks of the year? You need that hunger and passion to make an impact and get the results and job satisfaction you want. If you nibble at something, it will be less fulfilling. Look for a cause, a passion, interest or aspiration which really hits the spot.

What impact will they have for your own personal benefit?

Do you consider personal career success to be reflected in a healthy bank account, flashy car and exotic holidays? Or is it more about doing something great for the good of society or a charity – the feel-good factor is more important than pay and a wealthy lifestyle.

What do you want to do and what skills do you want to use to make these results happen?

As a biological science graduate, your university training will have given you many skills as you worked through lectures, seminars, tutorials, practicals, research projects and dissertations.

You've fine-tuned your laboratory and/or field-work skills and are well versed in safety, experimental design, hypothesis, testing, collecting results, record-keeping, critically evaluating and interpreting sound scientific data, writing up reports and essays, giving presentations, including reporting on data, and problem solving. You also have very specific skills which the modules and subject you've chosen to study have afforded you. You're able to solve problems in an analytical and logical way, and you're persistent, thinking of different ways to solve a mystery or problem, digging around for answers. You've developed skills in numeracy, project management, decision-making and team working. You work well on your own, and are used to autonomy, designing your own experiments and projects. You can pursue independent study and research, breaking tasks down into elements and following them while keeping track of deadlines. You can work under pressure,

Table 2.1

Achieving	Evaluating	Pricing
Acquiring	Finding solutions	Problem solving
Administering	Fundraising	Processing
Advising	Guiding	Producing
Analysing	Helping	Programming
Answering	Identifying	Project management
Applying	Implementing	Promoting
Assembling	Influencing	Qualitative skills
Assessing	Innovating	Quantitative skills
Building	Inspiring	Questioning
Buying	Interviewing	Recommending
Caring	Inventing	Researching
Challenging	Investigating	Revising
Classifying	Keeping records	Securing
Coaching	Leading	Selecting
Cold calling	Learning	Selling
Collaborating	Liaising	Servicing
Communicating	Listening	Setting targets
Conducting	Locating	Studying
Conserving	Making	Summarising
Consulting	Managing	Supervising
Counselling	Marketing	Supporting
Creating	Mentoring	Taking risks
Critical thinking	Monitoring	Talking
Dealing	Motivating	Teaching
Debating	Negotiating	Teamworking
Designing	Networking	Training
Detecting, e.g. false	Numeracy	Understanding
logic	Operating	Watching
Developing	Organising	Winning
Diagnosing	Persuading	Writing
Discovering	Planning	Other
Displaying	Preparing	
Distributing	Presenting	

and track information and compile the results and present them. You're skilled in using computers and retrieving information (data processing, graphics, word processing, email, web proficiency, library and internet searches).

In fact you'll have an array of skills, some of use to any employer (the transferable ones) and others to those in the science sectors. Table 2.1 gives examples of both transferable and job-specific skills.

Using the skills in Table 2.1 as a guide:

1   Which skills have you developed or practiced through your university life and academic studies? Build a picture around them.

2   Which would apply to any graduate of any discipline (i.e. are transferable)?

3   Look back to three achievements you are proudest of. Which skills did you use to make them happen?

4   Which skills do you want to use in future?

5   Which careers need those skills? For example, if you would like to communicate by telephone frequently all day, a career in head-hunting or sales may suit, as you need to do a lot of cold calling. If you enjoy writing, how about a career as a science writer?

Programmes such as Prospects Planner (www.prospects.ac.uk) can help you make the link between your skills and possible good career matches.

What sort of clients and customers do you want to work for?

This can affect the ethos and being of the organisation, be it private, public or voluntary sector. It can affect your pay, long-term working conditions and the sort of work you do. The *New Scientist Careers Guide 2007* shows the difference between industry and academia – study it if you are pursuing a career as a scientist. Some organisations are better on issues such as work–life balance than others. Potential employers could include:

- community
- government
- private sector
- charity
- international organisation
- yourself
- social enterprise
- dot.com
- micro-business (under five employees)
- small business (five to 49 employees)
- medium sized business (50 to 250 employees)
- large business (250 to 499 employees)
- corporate (500 plus employees).

The front-line client-focused role will have far greater liaison with external clients. Some professional service companies – such as recruitment agencies – focus on specific industries to build up a specialist knowledge of them, understanding trends, the career paths within them, changes, employer demands and the like. Many recruitment agencies specialise in a specific sector, such as science and technology. So consider who you want your clients and customers to be and the products you want to work with. They will impact on the people or organisations you deal with, perhaps one or several of the following:

1   Business/organisation to business/organisation, such as providing research and/or laboratory services.
2   Business to customer, in which case you're selling your company's goods to a customer, such as tutoring in biology courses.
3   Customer to customer, such as genetic counselling.
4   Public sector or voluntary organisations, or international bodies and governments, such as promoting a new health campaign.

Are there specific products or areas of expertise you want to work with?

Managing involves taking control of something, being in charge of it. The workplace is full of managers and there are opportunities for the specialist (finance, HR, facilities), or more of a generalist. Table 2.2 gives examples.

How do you see your career and lifestyle fitting in together?

Consider how your see your career and lifestyle intertwining and, importantly, how your career will impact on your loved ones.

Travelling to one conference after another to network with like-minded scientists may sound very exciting, and it can give you great experience, new friends, and the opportunity to collaborate on ideas, research and quests for knowledge, but it can also be quite lonely. Your absence can make a difference to the lives of loved ones you leave behind to handle the day-to-day running of the home, children, emergencies and their enjoyment of life. They will need

Table 2.2

Money, budgets	**Laws/regulations**
General management	Health and safety
Finance	Compliance
Accountancy	Company secretary
Banks, building societies	Human resources
Financial advisers	**Ideas**
People	Product development
Training and development	Design and creativity
Human resources	Advertising
Recruitment	Business development
Teaching	Innovation
Lecturing	Enterprise
Training/coaching	**Products**
Targets	Marketing
Recruitment	Product development
Sales	Distributing
Customer service	Buyer
Processes	**Systems**
Product development	Information technology
Disaster management	Disaster management
Distribution manager	**Words/language**
Events/Conferences/Exhibitions	Journalism
Selling	Publishing
Organising	**Buildings**
Advertising	Facilities management
Services	Health and safety
Marketing	Operations management
Customer service	
Insurance	

to be strong characters who understand your quest for knowledge, the importance of networking and working long hours. You, in turn, will need to stop and listen to concerns they have and find a way, between you, to work out compromises and solutions to situations you are finding stressful.

When you consider your career, do any of the following appeal?

- Travelling all the time, e.g. sales rep continually on the road – *Sales rep for a pharmaceutical company.*
- Working in another country with an occasional visit home? – *Anything you want to be!*
- Working with people of different cultures and customs – *International health organisations, such as the World Health Organisation.*

- Working for a company which will give you the opportunity to work abroad –
  University, research institute.
- Working for an international organisation –
  World Health Organisation.
- Helping under-developed countries, often working in very difficult and dangerous conditions –
  Voluntary Service Overseas, disaster management.
- Being the only person from your country –
  Volunteer, charity worker.

Consider the impact your career choice will have on your lifestyle – it can make a big difference on your quality of life.

What's of key importance to you in your career, whatever it is to be?

Identify the elements of work which matter to you in your life and career – Table 2.3 gives examples. Pinpoint three categories: which are essential to you, which are important, and which ones are the nice-to-haves? Do your choices reflect your own values? What does that tell you about your future career?

Moving your self-awareness forward

Your next step is to find out as much as you can about each sector you are interested in working for to uncover the real range of employment opportunities within it, including the pros and cons, so that you know what you're letting yourself in for. The sector's

Table 2.3

Motivation	Work for me rather than anyone else
Use of biological science skills	Results/outcomes
Purpose of work	Independence
Location	Entrepreneurship
Contribution to organisation/world/ sector/individuals	Personal fit – feeling that you belong? Skills you use
Sector – matching interests and knowledge	Values, as you identified in Chapter 1 Fit with lifestyle
Rules, ethics and behaviour	Knowledge you use
Role	Creativity
Rewards	Fun
Work – life balance	Using my degree subject to the full

professional body or trade association will be a good place to start; Chapter 4 outlines what it can do for you. Useful Addresses and Further Information will direct you to places where you can access further information. Use information worldwide – it can all help create a picture. For example:

1   How do your passions relate to the sectors you are most interested in and their niche areas? Who is working on them and which companies are involved? Which universities and research institutes are very involved in them?

2   How much do you know about the biological science sector in its widest form? Are there any areas which excite you but which you don't know much about? Which professional bodies and websites can tell you more about them?

Useful starting points include:

- The Prospects website is a mine of invaluable information on all graduate careers, including a complete empathy with the fact that you may choose to work in a sector unrelated to your degree. It has an excellent postgraduate website (www. prospects.ac.uk).
- The Association of Graduate Careers Advisory Services occupational profiles and booklets, such as *Science Sector* and *Environmental, Food Chain and Rural* (www.agcas.org.uk).
- *New Scientist* has an excellent careers guide which it updated in 2007, with salary and perk checks and comparisons (industry vs academia), employer profiles, thoughts from scientists on how they feel to ... win a Nobel prize, change the way the world thinks, see their research thrust into the public eye and more. You can download it for free (www.newscientist.com)
- The American Institute of Biological Sciences has a booklet called *Careers in Biology* (www.aibs.org/careers).
- The American Association for the Advancement of Science (AAAS) New Wave has lots of information geared towards graduate students and undergraduates. It has useful tips on resumes, networking, interviewing, etc. plus job listings, largely academic and research oriented, news, meetings, events, funding, careers fairs, workshops and more (http://sciencecareers.sciencemag.org).

- The Royal Society has case studies and comments from researchers on life as a scientist and the elements of their career that they enjoy (www.royalsoc.ac.uk).
- To get a tickle for postgraduate work, read some of the case studies at www.realworldmagazine.com, where you can find out why individuals chose to do a PhD, find out about their current job, what made them choose the career they did and what their job search strategy was. Learn from those who have gone before.
- Your own department, where you can get a rough idea of what past students have done after graduation. Refresh your mind by reading their case studies.

Create a vision or goal as a way to move forward

Once you've started to work out where you want to be and what you want to be doing, create your own goal, desired result – whatever you choose to call it – and give it some focus and specifics so that you can move your life and efforts in that direction. What is pulling you towards that career? Write up your goal or aim as specifically as you wish to help you focus, and remind yourself of it daily. Talk about what you want to do – as opposed to what you don't. Give it a time-limit, so that you have something to work for. Finally, make it sufficiently challenging to stretch you, but realistic. Break down what needs to be done into bits, so that you can work out what needs to be done when, step by step.

An example of a long-term career goal is:

In three years' time, I will:
➢ be working for ...
➢ have paid off 40 per cent of my student debt
➢ built up a network of friends in London I really feel I know well.

In six months' time, I'll have:
➢ researched all the firms I want to apply to
➢ found out what I need to do to qualify
➢ made the necessary networking contacts
➢ attended my first job interview.

Ask the right high-quality questions and you're more likely to get high-quality answers.

A word on family expectations

Family can particularly play a key role in our future career planning, unfortunately sometimes to the detriment of our own judgement of what is right for us. *'I went into it to please my parents'* often means that graduates went into safe, respected careers which met with nods of approval and sighs of relief from their loved ones, but made them, the graduate, feel they were en route to jail for a working lifetime. Today, most families are more relaxed about career choice (*'You can't tell them – they make their own minds up'*) usually voiced with all the inference that they still know better. They want us to be safe, protected, happy and successful, and a misunderstanding of the job market and a tendency to take on board negative messages from the media around us make things worse. There's nothing like the unknown and misunderstood to make people select the safe and known. While our friends and family have our interests very much at heart, their own agendas, self-interest and experiences may colour their well-meaning advice to us. They know our qualities well, but may have a limited experience and knowledge of the job market. Pinpoint a couple of practical ways they could help so that at the least they feel as though they are doing something.

If your family and friends have not gone through the process of higher education and have been in lower level jobs, seek to engage with people who are now in the career roles you aspire to, i.e. in the place where you want to be. Keep your sights high.

Summary action points

Bringing all the answers to the exercises in this chapter together:

1   What sort of a picture of my future career is emerging? What am I doing in it?
2   What information do I need to firm this picture up?
3   What do I need to happen next to help me further my career plans?
4   What do I need to know to start making decisions?

Chapter 3

Working out the 'how to'

This chapter is all about the 'how'. How will you get to where you want to be? What could you do to reach the outcome you want? What will you do to position yourself to be in a strong position to make the life you want happen? You will need an understanding of what is required of you from employers and/or course selectors, namely:

1   Technical experience, knowledge and understanding and skill; this depends on how relevant your degree was to the career you plan to follow. If it is directly relevant, you need to show that you can master the knowledge and research skills required for the role you want.
2   Business acumen, organisation and commercial awareness, plus an understanding of how organisations work.
3   Personal skills, such as leadership, management, the ability to plan your time, etc. – the transferable skills mentioned on page 21.
4   The passionate, go-getting approach to make it happen!

You also need a plan to help you smooth the path forward, so that you know what you're doing. Enter our five-point plan:

1   *What do you need to achieve your career goals, or at the least, your next step?*
    Find out by making good use of employers, careers advisers, professional bodies, trade associations, societies, young professionals who are where you want to be and your tutors.
2   *How far have you got in achieving your goal?*
    You may have already taken steps such as acquiring work experience, taking a degree course which grants you exemption

from the early stages of a professional qualification, finding
which universities offer the best opportunities for you at PhD
level and so forth.

3   *What have you done to position yourself to boost your chances
    of success?*
    This may involve activities such as:
    • relevant work experience to your career
    • undertaking an internship or work experience scheme
    • electing to go on to study a postgraduate qualification
    • joining the student branch of a professional organisation
    • attending professional meetings, campus presentations and
      careers fairs
    • focusing on what you want and committing energy and
      time to ensure you get it.

4   *What else do you need to do to attain your career goal?*
    Figure 3.1 shows possible steps to take. These may all feature
    at some time in your working life, alone or in combination.
    They may just appear as an opportunity too good to miss.
    Your decision to acquire professional qualifications depends
    on how committed you are to your chosen career path.
    This chapter will look at some of these options.

5   *How are you progressing to get to where you want to be?*
    This involves considerable action on your part, including:
    • Creating an action plan with timescales, to incorporate
      researching your options, meeting people and networking,
      sending in applications, attending careers fairs and
      presentations, and updating your CV.

Figure 3.1

- Being clear about what you want so that you don't waste time following up things which aren't really of interest.
- Giving your career the prominence in your life and the attention it deserves.
- Undertaking a learning audit, so that you are clear about what extra learning you need, be it on a formal (involving further study for academic or professional qualifications) or informal basis (attending a course on CV writing, learning more about the sector you want to have a career in).
- Where appropriate, finding out what you need to do to enrol for professional qualifications.

Consider also whether you want to have a break from the serious side of life and do something wild and wacky for a few months, such as travelling or taking time out. Is there anything else you would like to do for your own personal fulfilment and voyage? If the answer to either of these is 'yes', put them in context in terms of their importance and urgency in your life overall. Where do they fit now?

There is plenty of help available to you, so make the most of it. Professional bodies, learned societies, funding bodies, central government, higher education research associations, regional development agencies, careers services and research councils all have a part to play in helping you.

To be ... a postgraduate or not?

There has been strong growth in doctorate completion in the main subject areas of biological sciences (117 per cent increase) according to the Higher Education Statistics Agency. Indeed, the completion rate in science, engineering and technology overall rose by 88 per cent between 1994/5 and 2003/4, showing that more students are taking further qualifications to boost their expertise and skills. Those in physical and biological sciences were the largest groups. Studying for a postgraduate degree will enhance your knowledge, take your expertise to another level and boost your research and IT skills.

There are a range of postgraduate courses. You could, for example, choose to follow research-based studies, such as the PhD (Doctor of Philosophy), which take about three or four years full time to complete. A Masters in Research could be a first step, giving you a greater grounding in research skills and understanding the context and ethics around the subject. Increasing numbers of employers want graduates at this level and it can make a difference as to the level you enter the world of work at – unless, of course, you decide to stay on in the academic world. There is a New Route PhD which includes a number of taught units in the first two years and gives you a range of skills and techniques to help your research, enhancing your understanding of the management and commissioning of research. It will give you better teaching skills and prepare you if you wish to go into university as a leader or supervisor, but will also give you extra skills, should you decide to enter business. You can find out more about the New Route PhD at www.newroutephd. ac.uk.

A course that will enhance your career progression, such as the MBA, may suit you if you have already had a couple of years' work experience or you're looking to acquire a broad grounding in a subject. Equally, you may prefer to follow a taught postgraduate degree, which could cover any one of a range of subjects, including management, marketing, human resources, finance, banking, accounting and recreational management.

Some employers sponsor employees through degree and post-graduate courses and may even have a university create a bespoke course and qualification for their employees, but many people also study for a postgraduate degree for their own (career) development part-time. Do take note, however, that a stint of work experience may also be a route forward. What difference will a course make to the level you may start work at? A first degree will give you some responsibility and a junior role doing lab-based work; but if you have a higher degree, you will also enjoy higher levels of autonomy and responsibility in developing a project.

One other option is to work first before doing postgraduate study. This is particularly the case if you are going into a career which involves something like management, where a good stint of work experience will enhance your overall contribution to and benefit from the course. Timing is tricky; leave it too long and it may be too late to put impetus and fresh energy into your career.

Questions to ask before you sign up for a postgraduate degree are:

1 *What are my motivations for taking such a course?*
   Are you thinking, entry into a new career, career progression, research skills to go on? Ask yourself questions such as:

- What impact could it have on my career immediately after completion and five years down the line?
- What will it do for my standing internationally?
- How could it open doors for me?
- How does this course take me closer to achieving my long-term career plans?
- Where does it fit within them?
- What have postgraduate students gone on to do after their studies?
- How do these paths relate to my aspirations?
- Will a postgraduate degree substantially boost my chances of success?
- Will it really give me an edge over my competitors?
- What do employers think?
- What evidence do I have that postgraduate study will enhance my employment prospects?
- Will it enable me to change track from biological sciences to an entry point I'm happy with in a new career?

2   *What do I want to study?*
Considerations here are:
- What questions do I want answered?
- How will I research and study this material and do I love my subject enough to spend the one to four years on it every single working day?

Really challenge yourself on this one. How passionate are you, truly and honestly, about your chosen subject area? How much of your day does it occupy your thoughts and brain? Do you love it, breathe it, read about it at every opportunity – or is it more of an interest which has a lighter level of interest? Has your interest in and passion for the subject got what it takes to make the distance? How did current students know they had what it took?

3   *What will it take to be a successful applicant and student?*
How does postgraduate work differ from that at undergraduate level? What's different about the management and organisation of, say, a PhD to a BSc? How does the day-to-day routine differ, the contact with tutors, supervisors, professors, fellow students, the outside world? What determines your development throughout your studies and who will help you drive them? What form of assessment is there and how will you handle

that? Talk to your current tutors about your plans – do they think you have what it takes to be a successful postgraduate student? What skills will you need to be successful?

4 *What support will I need and what support will I get?*
What are the costs and what funding is available to you? Talk to current postgraduate students, your tutors, heads of departments or schools, employers and professional bodies. Visit any other university you're thinking of doing the PhD or other postgraduate course at to find out about facilities in laboratories, libraries and personnel. Meet your intended supervisor. Find out what you can about the strength of the department, its funding arrangements and links with employers and the outside world. Examine the research interests of the academics in the department carefully.

5 *What can I do to sell the benefits of a postgraduate degree to an employer?*
Many employers have enough problems understanding the benefits of an undergraduate degree, never mind the focus, rigour and academic discipline required to do a postgraduate one. What will you learn and how will a postgraduate course boost your research skills and subject expertise and understanding? What difference will such learning make to potential employers?

6 *Is it really a postgraduate course I need?*
Be very honest with yourself. Would another form of study and learning be more appropriate for the skills and knowledge you seek? Could networking and getting the right experience under your belt, perhaps by doing an internship, be as effective? Are you simply contemplating postgraduate study simply to put off joining the working world for another year? (*The longer you leave it, the harder it may be.*) What do you really want?

For more information on postgraduate studies

You'll find lots of resources listed under Useful addresses and further information, but meantime, the official UK postgraduate database at www.prospects.ac.uk lists the different courses available by subject, region and institution in the UK. You can apply online through Prospects. In the UK, apply as soon as you can because the more popular courses fill up early on – this means often October or

November in the year before the course is due to start. The National Postgraduate Committee (www.npc.org.uk) represents the interests of postgraduate students in the UK.

If you live outside the UK, the British Council (www.britishcouncil. org) has worldwide offices where staff can give you information about studying and living in Britain. You can access the British Science Council from its pages to find out all the latest news and efforts to enhance research collaboration, access its global science network and learn more about its science vision. The National Academic Recognition Information Centre (NARIC, www.naric. org.uk) provides a service for international students who want information on the comparability between international and UK qualifications.

Delve deep into your heart and brain to ensure that a postgraduate degree is the right thing for you to do. It could be that other ways forward would take you to where you want to get to without the financial and time costs.

For researchers from outside the UK ...

Don't forget Network UK (www.britishcouncil.org/eumobility), a fantastic resource aimed at science researchers planning to move to the UK. The website has practical information about visas, work permits, language courses and more, as well as latest science research news.

Also visit the European Union's 7th Framework Programme for Research and Technological Development (FP7) programme, which has a total budget of over €50 billion to give research grants out to individuals and teams. Visit http://cordis.europa.eu/fp7/home-en.html.

Enrolling for professional qualifications

You could study for professional qualifications relevant to your proposed career path to acquire the core knowledge and competences required to perform effectively at work. In some industries, you cannot advise clients or practice without them. If you join a large graduate employer, these may be part and parcel of the deal of signing up. They generally involve sitting for a number of examinations and practical experience and are on offer online, by evening class, through block learning or distance learning. Professional bodies have a list of accredited training providers and usually offer various support mechanisms to help you through. If you want to study for a qualification abroad, find out how your home country would view your intended course and qualification. The reference section of www.hero.ac.uk lists lots of professional bodies.

Short courses may be just the ticket

A short course may boost your employability and give you the skills you need to get that post you want or bounce you into that new career. Many of these are listed at www.hotcourses.com and www. learndirect.co.uk; local colleges and private training companies are also worth following through. Courses should be very practical to give you confidence and practice, and the course tutors should also have strong and current contacts with employers in the sector. A career development loan may just provide you with the finance you need to fill that vocational skill gap and boost your employability – visit www.direct.gov.uk/EducationAndLeaning/index.htm for more information.

You may, of course, be working already

Look back to the reasons why you enrolled for a degree, undergraduate or postgraduate. Perhaps you did so with your employer's knowledge, blessing and support. If this is the case, discuss your future with your employer, your direct boss or HR or both.

Questions to ask yourself at home are:

* What do I want to happen next?
* How can I use my new found knowledge and skills to boost my personal effectiveness now and to prepare me for the next stage in my career?
* Where do I see my career going in the next five years? How has this goal changed since starting my studies?
* What do I need to do now to make this happen?
* How has my new degree status changed my CV and what I have to offer?
* If I were to re-write my CV for my next perfect role, what would be missing from where I am now and that new description? How likely is it that I can make that happen at my current company?

- How do I see myself doing this: with my current employer, with another employer or starting up alone?

Whatever you choose to do, stretch your new confidence and intellectual prowess.

Going it alone

Self-employment is not the rosy picture it often appears. Many small companies are being strangled by red tape and the compensation culture, and it can be lonely. Consider how you'll handle tasks such as planning your business's vision, writing a business plan, setting yourself financial targets, dealing with health and safety issues, accounting and financial responsibilities, taking on staff and keeping to the right side of the law, keeping the books and records, ongoing business development, product and service development, dealing with the taxman, accountant and suppliers.

You could buy a franchise or set yourself up as a freelance, offering services and products by an hourly or daily rate. A franchise is a tried and tested product or a business selling products. The British Franchise Association (see Useful Addresses and Further Information) is the only independent accreditation body for franchising in the UK. Franchises cover a wide range of areas from pet care to refill printer cartridges, accountancy and taxation services to training centres. There are also workshops and seminars to give you lots of advice and tips on choosing a franchise and running a successful business. Before you buy any franchise, check its financial status and insist on seeing the accounts from its head office.

Develop an idea, create a vision, do your homework to research the market thoroughly, and make your decision.

Consider:

- What do you want your business to achieve? What do you want it to do?
- What will it look like in five years' time?
- What financial targets will it meet in six months', one year, three years and five years?
- Who will your customers/clients be? Where will they come from?

- What will your unique selling points be? What niche do you intend to focus on?
- What position will you take in the market?
- What brand do you want? What values will your business portray?
- What will your reputation be based on?
- What message and language can you use to grab potential customers' attention?
- What story would a SWOT analysis give you? (This involves identifying the Strengths, Weaknesses, Opportunities and Threats facing your business.) How does that analysis compare with your competitors in the market?
- What can you do to give your product or service that extra special added value, or to please and surprise your customer or client?
- Where will you run the business from?
- How will running a business impact on your lifestyle?

There will also be operational questions to ask such as:

- What funding do you need right now to set up and give yourself an income?
- How will you structure the business (e.g. limited company, sole trader, partnership)?
- How will you market your products and services?
- How will you price them?
- What equipment will you need to get started?
- How soon can you get up and running?

If you don't know how to go about any of these things, remember that university has given you the ability to *find them out*. There is a lot of advice and help about, from innovative centres where you can hire an office and share facilities at inexpensive rates, to advice from business advisers, events and online websites designed to help you make all the right decisions. Networking clubs enable you to talk to fellow entrepreneurs and help each other. In September 2004, Chancellor Gordon Brown launched the National Council for Graduate Entrepreneurship (www.ncge.org.uk). It in turn has set up Flying Start (www.flyingstart-ncge.com) which offers access to mentors and entrepreneurs, a funding database, expert advice and courses. Find out, also, what support your university offers graduates who want to start up their own business.

Biding time

Many people take any job to put food on the table while they are working to secure the first foothold into the career they want. Temporary work offers flexibility (but no guarantee of regular income) and it will enable you to build up a web of potentially useful contacts. Divided loyalty between your day job and trying to get a business off the ground or job hunt can be stressful and you'll need to manage your time and energy with care.

Don't lose your ambitions and aspirations while temping or working part time

1   Create a vision, a mission, a goal, perhaps a niche; be clear about what you want to do.
2   Break down into manageable chunks, so that every time you achieve a chunk, you feel that you're really making progress to your overall goal.
3   Be prepared to consider routes which might not necessarily demand a degree.
4   Give yourself a time-scale.
5   Ensure that you're giving this goal the prominence in your life that it truly deserves.
6   Be clear about how important it is to you.
7   Understand what it will cost you if you don't achieve it.

'I want to work abroad!'

Working abroad gives you a tremendously different outlook to those who have not been so fortunate to experience such an opportunity. Recruitment companies which have an international reach often have advice on their websites about moving abroad. Information on working in China, Taiwan, Thailand, Hong Kong, Singapore, Malaysia, Indonesia and Japan with market trends and industry summaries, and overall regional outlooks, plus details of events in the area can be found at www.asia.hobsons.com. Prospects (www.prospects.ac.uk) has numerous country profiles, incorporating details on the job market, international companies in the region you're reading about, language requirements, work experience, vacancy sources and visa and immigration information. Working abroad requires considerable research and preparation if you're to have the experience you want – they all vary greatly. Further reading at the end of this book has useful suggestions.

Eight questions to take into account are:

1 What do you want to get out of the experience?
2 Where do you want to work? Do you want to take the opportunity to learn a new language or improve existing language skills?
3 What do you want to do? Do you want to work for an employer in a job which will contribute to your career progression or simply go apple picking for six months?
4 How different do you want the culture of the country you're going to work in to be from your own?
5 How will your current qualifications be regarded in the country you plan to work in – will you need to get any additional 'top up' qualifications to meet their own regulations and criteria to work as a practising professional?
6 What visa requirements will there be? What happens about health insurance? What are the tax implications for you while working abroad and when you return home?
7 Can you do it under the auspices of your current or a future employer?
8 How long do you want to do it for?

Time out for golden sands, sea, sun ...

If you've been on the academic treadmill all your life without a break, you may feel like it's time for some time out, fun and rest. It's worth remembering that people of all ages take time out and more (larger) employers are offering sabbaticals to employees. They like seeing them return to the workplace refreshed, with a new confidence, fresh ideas, great soft skills and creativity. Gap programmes are also waking up to the fact that more of us want time out, and providing excellent opportunities for voluntary work and travel. Some charities offer the opportunity to do this for as little as a week, plus, you don't have to take a year out. If, however, you feel a year away would be just the ticket, visit www.gap-year. com, and for voluntary opportunities abroad, www.i-to-i.com.

That said, you live your life once. The moment you stop experiencing such adventures as travel and facing challenges in life, you stop living and start existing. If you plan to take some time out, you job hunt before you go and negotiate a start date for when you return (assuming you will return); or you could travel and look for a job when you get back. This gives you more flexibility and possibly more stress as you wonder how you'll find a job and pay off your debts when you get home.

Unemployment ...

Not a very inspiring option, is it? So get busy.

Seven ways to pass the time while you're unemployed:

1 Get relevant work experience, even if it's just for a week or a couple of days a week over a month or so.
2 Do voluntary work.
3 Learn new skills.
4 Travel.
5 Job hunt persistently and seriously – spend 40 hours a week on it.
6 Do something quite mad and quirky to make your CV stand out.
7 Study for a qualification which will give you on-the-job skills.

Getting nostalgic

Acknowledge that this is a difficult time, because you've worked hard towards your degree, celebrated in style, promised with complete strangers you met in the Union Bar in the last 24 hours at university that you'll keep in touch ... and suddenly, it's all over. And it's a strange feeling, so note its presence and then turn your attention to the future.

Give your life a turbo-boost!

If you're currently sitting at home with no clear future plans, climb out of your aimlessness and start walking purposefully to where you want to be:

1 Use of the careers support in your area.
2 Search out professional organisations which will give you the introductions you need.
3 Talk to fellow graduates. How could you support each other?

4   Build up a clear picture of the sector you wish to go into and be clear about how your skills, strengths and interests will contribute to it.

5   Talk to people in the sector by going to where you know they will be, such as trade exhibitions, local networking events.

6   Brainstorm strategies you can use which will boost your chances of success, such as a willingness to move and live where the sector is strongest.

7   Find out what is going on to encourage graduates to work for small and medium sized companies.

8   Set yourself daily targets and goals in every area of your life, not just your career. Life isn't just about work. Do things which make you feel good about yourself.

Summary action points

Move your thinking forward:

1   Who do I need to talk to in order to find out which entry routes are available to me?

2   What steps will I take next and how will they move me closer to my goals? What do I need to do to make them happen?

3   Which university or college runs the course in the subject I'm looking for?

4   What funding is available for me to set up my own business?

5   What initiatives are available that might be relevant to me and my career goals?

6   What do I need more of in my life right now? How can I get it?

Chapter 4

Connecting with your network

The world's a network

Connecting to those in the know who can help you move closer to the things you want in life will enable you to enjoy a far richer life and career. Chapters 4 and 5 will help you pinpoint people who can help you create or open doors to new opportunities.

A strong, active network can lead you straight to decision-makers and in turn enable you to reach out, help others and live a highly successful and fulfilling life. Whatever stage of life and career you are at, a lively network will enhance your prospects of obtaining the introductions you need. Highly successful people have a network of business associates, acquaintances, colleagues and friends they can turn to for information, advice, introductions and help. You create your own luck and networks in life, however, and they are as active and useful and productive as you make them. And remember that networking is also about helping those who *have* helped you, and those who *haven't*. In the world of science, a network is crucial to enable you fully to collaborate, share ideas, research, experience the joy of discovery and the frustrations of near-results.

This chapter considers the 'who' question in a networking capacity.

- Who can help me?
- Who can give me the support I need now?
- Which websites will be most useful?

Eight steps to networking well are:

1   An ability to chat and be really interested in the other person; you need to be able to establish rapport with strangers quickly.
2   Listening and questioning skills.

3 A get up and go attitude – go out there and fight for your place in the world.
4 Follow through. Dump the information you acquire, file it for future thought or action it but *do* something with it.
5 Lateral thinking – does your contact know of anyone else you should talk to?
6 Respect! The person you're talking to has got to where they are by hard work. They believe in what they are doing and in what the job stands for. It may not turn out to be your niche or world, but respect them for what they love about theirs.
7 Being nosey and curious.
8 Accept feedback calmly.

You may not always like what you hear. *'This is a very tough industry and not many people make it'*. Okay, so that may be the case, but clearly people *do* make it, so focus on the percentage that do succeed – the 5 per cent, 10 per cent, 20 per cent of applicants – and find out just what it is that brings them success, rather than generalisations such as, *'It's difficult, it's tough'*. It may well be difficult, but it's not impossible. Turn the negatives around to: *'It's difficult, but it's possible. It's tough but it's rewarding'*. Talk about the *'I can'* and *'I will'* rather than the *'I'll try'* or *'Maybe …'*. Ask people *'What is your perception of me?'* to get feedback on how you present yourself and how you come over. This will help give them something to remember you by. *'I met with a journalist who was absolutely passionate about … really great ideas and done some terrific projects. You should give him a call – might be able to help you …'*.

What would the cost be to you if your career goals *didn't* happen? Envisaging such an outcome can be a highly effective lever to get you out of your thinking zone and into a doing one, making calls and sending emails. It can propel you into going the extra mile and turning just one more corner to find the right opening. What are you willing to do to make sure your career happens? How outlandish are you prepared to be and how far out of your comfort zone are you prepared to go? Your passion for your career and what you want to achieve should inspire and excite you so much that you're prepared to do what it takes to sell yourself. True networking is only really effective when you push yourself out of your comfort zone and make the effort.

A key benefit to your networking activities will be to create and build a strong support team around you. Each person on your team should bring you something different. There will be members of your support team you've known all your life, such as your family, family friends and your friends. Within that group, there will be one or two people whom you trust perhaps just that bit more than the rest. You know they will be open and honest with you and you also know you handle any constructive criticism from them because it's fair and just. Then there are people who fill you with energy, a can do approach, who inspire you to great things. Perhaps these may include your peers at university; how often have you sat about and brainstormed an idea late into the night? Keep in touch with those friends who enable you to unlock your potential and your creativity. There will also be the people you (secretly) admire and consider your success and role models. They may be a member of your family, perhaps your mother or father, or a high profile leader in business, politics, the community, or someone whose go ahead approach fills you with energy and passion for your own beliefs and causes. Bring these people on board by studying their methods to achieve success. What did they sacrifice along the way to get to where they wanted to be? How did they focus? Why not contact them to ask them how they did it and what advice they have for you? Would they act as a mentor to you? Finally, there are those who are not yet known to you – those people working in the sort of profession you want to be in, those who can advise you and help you along the way. And it is here that the skill of networking truly comes into its own.

The benefits of networking

Networking is all about asking others to help you access information which will help you – or others – get to where you need to be, enabling you to tap into those who are most likely to provide you with the answers you need. To reach them, you will have to go beyond the people you know and extend out a call for help to those you *don't*.

This is the same in life. We all need the right people to call on in moments of crisis because we know they will give us the right support at that moment. We choose our friends because they have qualities we admire and enjoy. We elect to take some family members into our confidence as opposed to others because we know they have something slightly different to offer us, perhaps due to their life experience or their approach or attitude. As we go through life, we'll call on people at different times and there will be periods when we aren't in touch at all. Nonetheless, keep those fires of warmth and support burning because we know that when the time comes, we'll need to know we can pick up the telephone and call them or drop them an email to ask for help, even if it's just a friendly ear. Just the same way, there are people who know they can call on us.

Let's consider how networking can help you in your career. If you brainstorm all the people you know, who you've met or watched at presentations as they came into your university, you can probably draw up one heck of a list as Figure 4.1 shows.

Do you feel comfortable talking to strangers and establishing a rapport with them? You should: you've done it before at university!

Fifteen ways networking can help you in your career:

1   Acquiring relevant work experience, especially in highly competitive sectors where contacts are everything.
2   Help with your CV, application or portfolio.
3   Information about a career or organisation, or better still, an introduction to someone working in it.
4   An idea of the skills, qualities and experience an employer wants and the personalities they recruit; would you be a good 'fit'?
5   How a sector works, e.g. the culture, behaviour, dress, language, values.
6   The name of the best recruitment agency for you to talk to.
7   Advice on the best way 'in' to a sector or company.
8   Projects an employer needs doing but does not have the resource internally to undertake which you could then volunteer for.
9   Tip offs when a job comes up – many companies advertise their vacancies to staff first on their notice boards or company intranet.
10 What roles are available for new graduates?
11 Where is the best place to look for vacancies?
12 Discussing the industry overall, its strengths, weaknesses, opportunities and threats; the pros and cons of working in it and how it is structured.
13 Advice from small business owners as they reflect back on their own experiences of setting up. Did they make any mistakes they would warn others about?

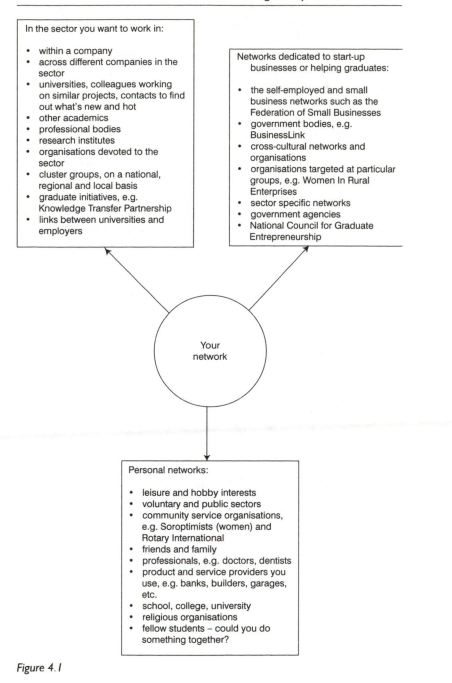

In the sector you want to work in:

- within a company
- across different companies in the sector
- universities, colleagues working on similar projects, contacts to find out what's new and hot
- other academics
- professional bodies
- research institutes
- organisations devoted to the sector
- cluster groups, on a national, regional and local basis
- graduate initiatives, e.g. Knowledge Transfer Partnership
- links between universities and employers

Networks dedicated to start-up businesses or helping graduates:

- the self-employed and small business networks such as the Federation of Small Businesses
- government bodies, e.g. BusinessLink
- cross-cultural networks and organisations
- organisations targeted at particular groups, e.g. Women In Rural Enterprises
- sector specific networks
- government agencies
- National Council for Graduate Entrepreneurship

Your network

Personal networks:

- leisure and hobby interests
- voluntary and public sectors
- community service organisations, e.g. Soroptimists (women) and Rotary International
- friends and family
- professionals, e.g. doctors, dentists
- product and service providers you use, e.g. banks, builders, garages, etc.
- school, college, university
- religious organisations
- fellow students – could you do something together?

Figure 4.1

14   Names of bodies and groups which are really helpful when setting up a business.
15   Names of grants or funding you can tap into.

Many people don't push their network into unknown areas so never really truly reap the benefits networking can bring.

The danger of networking with fellow graduates is that if you're both in the same boat, you may simply spend time and energy bemoaning the current state you're in, which won't change anything. So if you're talking to a fellow graduate, have a good moan for five minutes and then spend 15 minutes brainstorming, during which time you can both change the situation you're in for the better and bounce ideas and contacts off each other. One of them could be the breakthrough you've been looking for. Figure 4.2 shows you just how.

Get pushy and politely ask for help. Most people will be delighted to help you.

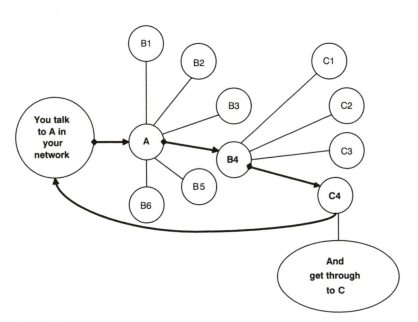

Figure 4.2

Six steps to proactive networking:

1   Identify what you need to know or what sort of people you want to meet and why they are important to you.
2   Identify the people you *do know* and imagine on paper what their network would be like.
3   Make contact and ask for advice and help. If someone has referred you to a contact, mention their name.
4   Approach people you don't know but can find more easily through relevant professional organisations and trade associations.
5   Think big and laterally and you could connect to thousands of people worldwide at a stroke. The key is to secure introductions to the people in the right place.
6   Be open to asking for advice and help.

Professional organisations

Professional bodies exist partly to help promote the public's confidence in the professions they represent. As such, membership of a professional body may be essential to practice. Many offer a ladder of steps to climb as you work your way up, acquiring professional qualifications from student level to fellow, or whatever term they use to describe the more senior-level personnel. They help members and new entrants into the field to have satisfying and fulfilling careers, access to the right training and networks, and meet the challenges and opportunities that come their way. Many such organisations in the biological sciences are listed under Useful addresses and further information, but you can pick up many more from www.worktrain. org.uk and www.prospects.ac.uk. Their websites may cover topics as demonstrated in Table 4.1. Whatever your career plans and whichever sector you choose to enter, you'll find professional bodies a wealth of practical, up-to-date information.

Most are sympathetic to the job seeker, especially those from college or university, or those returning to work. On initial contact, you may talk to a person employed by the professional body to be at the end of the phone, offering information and advice. They will have particular hints and advice for you, the new entrant, the career changer, the mature student, the young professional. They can also help point you in the direction of areas of their website which may be of interest and to local groups in your area. And membership

Table 4.1

• A register of practitioners and their areas of expertise and specialism, often with their contact details	• Career case studies
	• Learning and education
	• Useful links
	• Information about the profession as a whole
• Events taking place at which members, associates and affiliates may gather	• Library services
	• Annual conferences in the UK and abroad
• Jobs search	• Salary calculator
• Online forum groups	• Services available to the public
• Latest industry news	• Vacancy listings
• Latest publications relevant to the industry	• Advice line on pricing issues
	• Setting up on your own
• Research	
• Information for the public on the body, its standards, ethics and training	

may be essential if you want to practice as a professional. If you're considering joining a profession, find your way around its website. Many professional bodies are allied to international groups, thereby giving them a global view and contacts.

When visiting their websites, make good use of the links pages professional bodies provide. The Institute of Biology (www.iob. org), for example, has a number of affiliated societies which may be of equal interest and relevance to you; its website has details of UK branches, enabling you to find your nearest courses and events, which provide an excellent opportunity to meet people, plus consultation papers, policies and more. It has information on professional development with example summary forms of, for example, a research scientist. The Anatomical Society's website at www.anatsoc.org.uk has information about prizes, grants and more – some of which may provide you with an opportunity to attend meetings as a student – plus many more links to relevant societies, universities, useful research and news. It also has lots of research-related websites and education-related websites for different areas such as neuroscience and embryology.

Professional bodies' discussion forums are very useful to see what the hot topics are and to be able to comment on them at interviews or assessment days. It is not uncommon for people to ask for careers advice and point out that they are looking to move into an area, and for other professionals to come forth with advice and information. Many organisations have local networks, with regular meetings (sometimes with a speaker), events, training programmes and newsletters. There may also be visits to businesses and a look around, or a social gathering. Most will enable members to talk to each other and catch up, meet new people or give each other referrals. The Challenger Society for Marine Science (www. challenger-society.org.uk) holds events and meetings for young scientists and students, and acts as an educational and information point. If you are interested in ocean science, why not look it up and go along to a meeting?

Go on – attend a meeting in your area

It is in the club's vested interests to show you goodwill and interest and yours to represent yourself in a professional manner. Dress in business attire – suit and tie – and practice good social skills – a warm, firm handshake, a smile and lots of eye contact. Ask questions – what people do, who do they work for, what sort of clients do they have? If they give you their business card, follow it up with an email saying something like 'It was nice to meet you – would it possible for us to meet up – I'd love to talk you further about … '. Be ready to talk positively about your course, the research projects you did and that you are currently working on, your career plans and people who inspire you. Mention articles you've seen in the press or online which show you're up to date and show enthusiasm and interest. Find out before you go about any initiatives in your area which are running to strengthen the relationship between graduates and small employers – it could just help swing the mind of a small employer to give a graduate like you a chance, if only if he or she had some guidance on how to make the most of you.

If the thought of attending such a meeting fills you with horror …

Why not contact the person in charge of your local group to explain that you're coming along for the first time and to ask for someone to look out for when you arrive to introduce yourself? There should be someone there whose role it is to welcome new members and make them feel at home. Look out for them, and ask them to introduce you to someone who is working in a specific area that you'd like to get involved with. Find out in advance who will be there, and head for those you most want to talk to when you arrive, armed with prepared questions. Be interested and you'll soon forget your own nerves. Remember that you're with a group of like-minded people who will remember well what it's like to start out. They're on your side. Ask to meet them to find out more. Identify specific questions to ask before you go so that it is clear you have given the meeting some thought and prepared well for it.

Join your alumni

Do it now; you'll find details on your university's website. Try tracking down past alumni who are working in sectors you want to join. They can answer many of your questions, give you advice and may be able to point you in the right direction of more help and support. Find out what they like and dislike about what they're doing, and what they see the challenges are from the point of view of their career and life. What appealed about the organisation they joined and how has the partnership fared so far? Where do they see it going in the future? Why not set up an e-group of your fellow graduates to act as a focal point of ideas, contacts, support, advice and help?

Academic groups

Academics network across the world as much as professionals in the business field. They attend conferences, listen to papers, give presentations, undertake joint research projects, compare notes, research, debate, argue, discuss, discover and invent. They talk on the phone, they email and they have their own networks across their universities, research institutes and other relevant organisations. They live and breathe their subjects, and they're encouraged to work with business, whether they like it or not, and to create a far more entrepreneurial spirit in their departments and students. You could choose to be one of them. A number of academic associations exist, including the Heads of University Biological Sciences (HUBS); for more information, visit www.biology.leeds.ac.uk/HUBS/index.htm or check out the Inside HE section on the HERO website (www.hero.ac.uk).

You may be thinking that academic life is for you. Visit websites such as www.jobs.ac.uk and www.academicjobseu.com for information on jobs in the higher education sector and check institutions' own websites for vacancies. As well as academic posts, universities also need staff in areas such as finance, marketing, PR, administration, student support, HR and facilities and building management.

Worldwide networking, academic and otherwise

We have included many UK professional bodies, societies, academies and institutes in Useful addresses and further information – make the most of their link pages and you'll discover a considerable amount of extra resource.

There are three excellent websites which give you access to professional bodies, societies, institutes, universities and more between them. They are:

*   www.hero.ac.uk – website for Higher Education and Research Opportunities in the UK, which has many links to websites that could be of interest, together with an excellent section on research in the UK;
*   www.scholarly-societies.org – this fantastic Canadian project aims to facilitate access to scholarly societies worldwide. It is huge. Within biology and the environment, for example, you can find links relating to:
    *   general biology and the environment
    *   agriculture
    *   atmospheric and metereological science
    *   botany
    *   cell biology, cytology and histology
    *   ecology, biodiversity and conservation biology
    *   environmental sciences
    *   genetics and evolution
    *   microbiology, bacteriology and virology
    *   molecular biology
    *   soil science
    *   water science, hydrology, oceanology
    *   zoology.
    There are more websites relating to other subjects, including health and medicine listing country-specific websites, and those with a more international flavour; they all contribute to the opportunities for you to network with other bodies and access information on major issues affecting science, medicine, health and more. Examples are:

- The Council of Science Editors (US-based) (www. councilscienceeditors.org/);
- The Institute of Biological Engineers (www.ibeweb.org);
- The Federation of American Soceities for Experimental Biology (www.faseb.org);
- World Conservative Union (www.iucn.org);
- European Federation of Biotechnology (www.efb-central. org/).

From Canada to Australia, and China to Madrid, this amazing website (www.scholarly-societies.org) lists many societies – which in turn produce more through affiliates, links, professional associations and so on. The European Federation of Biotechnology, for example, serves biotechnologists across Europe, and is a non-profit association of all learned societies, universities, institutes, companies and individuals who are interested in the field. It has a job board, forums and yet more links to national biotechnical associations. The more you rummage and dig, the more you find!

- www.intute.ac.uk/healthandlifesciences is a goldmine of education and research resources.

What else?

You can access careers advice and information online and in person through a number of websites and these are listed under Useful addresses and further information through university careers services and government providers, plus websites such as www.prospects. ac.uk and www.get.hobsons.co.uk. These also have specific websites for postgraduates. Wherever you are, visit or contact your local university's careers service and find out what help is available to you as a new graduate. Be specific about the help you need. Know the questions you want answers to. Go into careers interviews knowing what you want to cover. Be honest with yourself and others – this is no test. In addition, there may be websites geared towards graduates in your particular region, such as GradSouthWest (www.gradsouthwest.com) in the south west of the UK (see Useful addresses and further information).

Websites can act as invaluable pointers to further websites which are worth investigating. Always check out their links pages.

Women

There are a growing number of websites catering for women and in particular women returners. For example, there are several websites and resources for women in science, engineering and technology, such as the UK Resource Centre for Women in Science, Engineering and Technology (www.setwomenresource.org.uk). It has advice and information, courses, help for those who are looking to return to work, role models, mentoring opportunities, careers information and more. There's also WISE, Women into Science, Engineering and Construction (www.wisecampaign.org.uk) and the Daphne Jackson Trust (www.daphnejackson.org) which seeks to help women returners.

Start-ups

There are also websites for the small business and start-ups, such as the Federation of Small Businesses (www.fsb.org.uk) , the Small Business Service, Start-Ups (www.startups.co.uk) and BusinessLink (www.businesslink.gov.uk). Some are very specific, such as Women in Rural Enterprises (WIRE) in the UK (www.wireuk.org).

Do it successfully

Open-mindedness and generosity is crucial, but can also be discerning. Listen to what people have to say, and then assess the information and feedback you're getting against what's important to *you* and your criteria.

Ten more steps to successful networking are:

1   Don't assume the information you're getting is current and that the people you're talking to are up to date. Check with professional bodies and trade associations.
2   Guard your safety. Meet people you don't know in a public place or in their office premises when others are around. Visit the company's website to ensure its address is valid. Don't give too many personal details out over the internet or telephone.
3   Present yourself at the highest standard possible using business behaviour and language. Examine yourself from head to toe in front of a long mirror in your interview suit. What image

do you want to portray? How far is your reflection a mirror of that image?

4   Use networking to digest strategies which will put you ahead, whether you're looking for a new job or starting and developing your own business.

5   Networking is a two-way process. When people help you, see if there is anything you can do to help them. Treat others as you would like to be treated yourself.

6   If you are at a networking event, spend five minutes talking to the person you're with and then move on. You are *all* there to meet as many people as possible, so close the conversation: *'It's been nice to meet you. Shall we exchange cards and move on?'*.

7   What perception do you want the people you meet to have of you? Do you want to come over as someone who takes their career and chosen field seriously and passionately, or as someone who's out to have a good time? Are you portraying yourself to be someone who can be trusted?

8   Don't give the impression you hop from one company to another. It costs employers money to recruit staff; word gets around if you job-hop, especially if you live in a small community or work in a small sector. Be discreet if you're looking elsewhere for opportunities.

9   Know what you want to achieve from each networking opportunity. Divide your networks in groups and give each group a goal for the week or month. Measure your success. What are you doing that is yielding the best results?

10   Keep in touch with people in your network. Email them from time to time to ask how they are and how things are going. A network is only as active and alive as you make it.

Go out there and immerse yourself in the fabric and make-up of those working in the sector you want to get into.

Build up a strong knowledge and understanding of the world you want to work in and seek to identify who really knows its scene and has an influence in it. Informal networks are as important as those which are of a professional foundation, so make the most of every opportunity to meet like-minded people who share the same passions you do, whatever sector you plan to work in. Informal networks are the places to go to meet people who will give you good, sound advice over a pint, talk about *the* latest work from the sector which is truly giving everyone the 'wow' factor. And tap into informal networks socially and laterally; an accountant could, for example, have a client in just the sector you're looking to work in and he could be willing to give you a name and make an introduction. Be chatty and interested, passionate and enthusiastic, keen and self-motivated and a great listener, and you'll attract help and support, but you also need to go out of your way to find it.

For the scientist, conferences will be hugely important places to network. Plot your attendance carefully and find out who will be attending in advance so that you can ensure anyone you particularly want to meet is on your list. Enjoy them too – you will come away feeling inspired, refreshed, ready for the challenge and reeling from the joy and wonder of being with people who are as fascinated by your subject and its endless possibilities as you are. Work out a way to keep in touch with those you meet and make the effort to do it.

Networking is for life!

Networking can be very helpful in all sorts of ways such as:

1   Finding specialist expert health advice.
2   Locating the estate agent who will really get your house sold fast and is always the first to hear of houses coming onto the market.
3   Getting your kids into the right school.
4   Looking after ageing relatives and making the system work to your advantage.
5   Volunteering to give something back.
6   Meeting people of like mind, such as knowing where the places are to go to meet fellow scientists.
7   Asking about hotels for that special holiday next year.
8   Meeting new people at the pub, in the gym, and through your interests.
9   Learning something new and keeping your life fresh and alive.
10 Having fun and giving something back at the same time.

Summary action points

The way you network at every level can affect the flavour and fabric in your life so make it a priority.

1   What network groups are there in your area which you can make contact with and get involved with? List them and make that first contact.

2   Find out if they have mentors to help people like yourself who want to get into the sector. If they do, ask if you can be allocated one.

3   Contact five people in your network. Ask if they know of anyone who could help you. Arrange to meet for a coffee to catch up with them or organise an information meeting.

Chapter 5

Hunting out that right opportunity

So far, you've ascertained what you want to do – now you need to work out how and where you want to do it. One factor to feature in is *where* you're going to be living.

How important is the 'where' to you?

What factors are driving your decision in terms of where you live? Many graduates move abroad to find the lifestyles and career opportunities they want – would you move to where the right career opportunities were for you tomorrow, regardless of where that was?

Other factors which will impact on your lifestyle are your access to cultural activities, sports and leisure interests, the make up of local people and quality of life in the area. You are unlikely to find somewhere which hits all of these criteria so some degree of compromise will be required. If your career matters to you above all else, you'll move to where the sector is strong and growing fast as opposed to where it is non-existent.

Whatever sector you work in, be alert to opportunity

Every sector has its hot spots and weak parts so depending on what you decide to specialise in, you'll need to be prepared to travel and move to where the action is, sometimes on a contract basis for a university, research institute or employer who needs expertise on the scene. Watch for trends in your chosen field carefully. Such tracking can open your eyes to opportunities you'd never dreamt of. Once you start looking and watching, it's amazing how many openings will come your way. If you can get to a conference, then go. Check to see if there are student rates, offer to do something for the conference in exchange for your fee, ask for a special student rate if there is none. Most professional bodies will have something to say about the changes taking place in their sectors. Your university may have access to websites and journals such as www.trends.com which has 15 journals covering biomedical and life sciences.

You can pick up more news, developments and information from websites such as:

1   *Nature* at www.nature.com/news/index.html
2   *New Scientist* at www.newscientist.com, including business trends
3   *Science News* at www.sciencenews.org/, a weekly magazine online
4   *Science* Daily at www.sciencedaily.org/ – a website of the latest research news of scientific breakthroughs with 15-minute updates
5   News from the AAAS at http://sciencenow.sciencemag.org/, including daily news from *Science*Now.

Once you have chosen the sector you wish to go into, bookmark its relevant bodies, journals and news websites so that you can get regular updates. Can you publish or comment on them to raise your profile? You'll find a considerable list of e-journals at www.e-journals.org/ covering a range of subjects, including the top 500 scientific journals, botany, public health, biochemistry and cell biology, oceanography, zoology microbiology and more.

What's the picture in the UK?

The expectation is that there will be significant increases in a demand for those at the higher skilled end of the work force, such as managers, professionals, associate professionals and those engaged in technical and service occupations. That said, each region has its growing industries and those in decline. You can find out where your sector's hot spots are by looking at government websites relating to trade and industry, the economy and websites such as the UK Trade and Investment at www.invest.uktradeinvest.gov.uk/ and the Office of Science and Innovation at www.dti.gov.uk/science/. Foresight may also be of interest at www.foresight.gov.uk/index.html.

In areas of traditional and declining industries, redundant skills and depleting resources, governmental Regional Development Agencies

(RDAs) (www.endglandsrdas.com) in England are responding by creating initiatives in such areas to regenerate them, boost learning opportunities and facilitate skill acquisition and start-ups. They have their equivalents in Scotland, Ireland and Wales, plus there are European RDAs (www.eurada.org). Government bodies such as the RDAs will tell you the sectors are expected to enjoy strong growth or experience a shrinkage – labour market intelligence can be very helpful. Cluster groups and localised graduate websites (see Further Reading) may direct you to useful local networks. Websites such as SEMTA at www.semta.org.uk has lots of information about sector strategy groups, labour market assessments, training frameworks and occupational standards, as do other sector skills councils which you can access from www.ssda.org.

What initiatives are available to encourage employers to take on graduates?

Governments are investing a lot of money in developing skills and talent, and particularly so at the graduate end of the market. There are many initiatives, programmes, events, websites, help-lines, networking groups, advisory services and more to help you and your peers. In the UK, for example, RDAs are encouraging universities and businesses alike to retain skilled talent in their area and working to raise small companies' awareness of how graduates can benefit them. There is a strong connection between the skill levels in an area and the quality of working opportunities and lifestyle on offer, which is why huge efforts are being made to regenerate the weaker areas. Consider initiatives such as the Knowledge Transfer Partnerships (www.ktponline.org.uk) which enable graduates and postgraduates to undertake a project within a company while acquiring management training at the same time. The initiative works to promote enterprise, creativity and innovation. Find out whether graduate apprenticeships operate in your region to help you make the step between university and employment. Don't forget internships and work experience programmes (see www.work-experience.org).

Many regional graduate careers service providers (see Useful Addresses and Further Information) offer work placement programmes and schemes designed to boost your employability. This forms part of their drive to encourage graduates to remain in the area after their degree studies. Tap into them because they will help smooth your path through offering workshops, initiatives, practical advice and information which could be the difference between you struggling on and getting there eventually or taking the fast track to success.

Don't forget regional and local government and bodies

Local government agencies and bodies can also give you labour market information and helpful hints as to what is going on in your area. Two examples are www.futureskillsscotland.org.uk and www.futureskillswales.com, which show cluster groups, links between education and industry, research and development areas, skills needed, plans for the regions and more. Enterprise agencies in the area may also have advice for those starting out, details of trade shows, training, events, help-lines, agencies and links. Find out what's happening in *your* area.

Analyse the sector you wish to join and consider the size of the average company in it

The size of the niche area or sector will make a difference as to how competitive it is to get into. You may need to move abroad to get entry into your desired career or into an allied industry in your home country if that's where you want to stay. The size of the niche area or sector will make a difference as to how competitive it is to get into. There may be 30,000 PR companies in the UK, for example, but 300,000 banks, so you could deduce that it will be more difficult to get into a PR company than a bank, particularly as many employers take graduates of any discipline.

Finding suitable employment opportunities

First, consider how much you know about the companies and organisations in the sector you are applying to:

1   Where do they tend to be based? Does one region of the country or world tend to have a monopoly?
2   Who are the companies in that sector? What size are they? What do they do? Who are their clients? What is happening in

that particular area to encourage large and small companies to take graduates and postgraduates on?

3   How do they recruit? Chapter 7 has more information on this. Are there recruitment agencies which have a track record of dealing with the sector and the area? Which agencies are they?

Employers use a range of methods to recruit employees and you should use a range of methods in your job hunting. Companies may work with links with your university department, approaching their academic contacts in it outside the usual round of careers fairs and presentations. They will probably use their own websites or those of agencies, advertisements in the local press, looking at on-spec applications, finding students through work experience, internships and secondments. Some employers take staff on through the temporary route, that is to say they advertise a temporary position first, see how the candidate works out and then, assuming all is well and that both websites find a good 'fit', offer the candidate a permanent post.

Having identified where you want to work, search out those employers!

Don't just use one method to job hunt and search out opportunities. Enlist several. Figure 5.1 below refers to job hunting, but you could equally create your own similar figure if you were going into academia.

In addition, you should:

1   Run a search for all the relevant employers using all the means at your disposal, including Kompass and Dun and Bradstreet.
2   Check out graduate listings such as Prospects Directory, Prospects today, Prospects Finalist, the Hobsons Directory and careers service listings.
3   Use your local library which should have sector reports, books and information about the local area, trade and national magazines, phone and trade directories.
4   Register for any email alerts with online agencies to pick up new jobs which come in that might interest you.

Take action

Plan; Search; Identify; Contact; Join; Find out; Ask; Enthuse; Listen; Create; Listen

Figure 5.1

Hint: you can do a search for businesses at http://local.google. com/. Use several search terms to maximise the effectiveness of your search.

Many online websites have job searches and vacancy listings, as do specialist trade journals such as the *New Scientist* (printed and online), *Nature, The British Medical Journal* and *The Lancet*. Find out which journals operate in the sector you propose to join; visit their websites or subscribe to their printed materials; find your way about them, and then bookmark them. Don't just limit your search to looking through job pages. If you see news of a company which interests you, visit its website and, if you like what you see, visit its careers or vacancies pages. If there are no relevant pages, there's nothing to stop you sending your CV on spec.

Go on the alert for vacancies

Of course you can register your details with various online agencies, associations and groups, which have the facility to enable employers to search out someone with the skills and talents they need. This enables you to receive email or mobile phone alerts when new jobs come in and to browse the vacancies available and make contact with the appropriate agency or employer. Online and printed directories can help you identify small and medium sized companies to consider. You can often register with websites for a fee and acquire access to hundreds of jobs with daily alerts and lots of great links and careers information. Keep your personal details up to date, so that they reflect any extra experience and skills you're acquiring. In addition, many websites list details of opportunities.

Going through recruitment companies

Recruitment agencies are selected by employers to find recruits for them. Many employers have long-standing relationships with agencies, so agency consultants build up an extensive knowledge of what the employer is like to work for and what sort of career path candidates can expect upon successful application and starting.

Agencies offer various services to their candidates, including help with CVs (although some agencies have their own particular CV format to send to clients); and profiling so that you can work out what sort of work would suit you best. Your consultant should have a clear idea of trends in the sector, and how your career will fit into it, and he or she should enjoy strong links with the industry. Many offer training, and some run networking evenings. It's essential to remember that your consultant is human, too, so treat him or her as you would like to be treated.

Online recruitment has become big business. Many online agencies and professional bodies offer the facility of receiving email alerts, enabling you to receive notice that new (relevant) vacancies are available. Newspapers and trade magazines also have online vacancy boards and often send newsletters. You may also be able to post your CV on some websites for potential employers to view.

If you want to get into a specific industry, look for agencies which are active in that industry and focus on it, with a good track record – they are more likely to have a strong network and an ear to the ground for opportunities. The Recruitment and Employment

Confederation has hints for job seekers and lists of agencies handling specific sectors – visit www.rec.uk.com for more details. You can quickly access a huge number of agencies in specific sectors by visiting www.agencycentral.co.uk which has both agencies and job sites listed by sector and also has a full list of agencies offering graduate positions. Examples of agencies are:

1   the Science Recruitment Group (www.srg.co.uk)
2   Matchtech (www.matchtech.com)
3   CSL Recruitment (www.cslrecruitment.com)
4   Camco Scientific (www.camcoscientific.com).

Go where the action is ready to sell your expertise and skills

This includes careers events and trade fairs. Many events will provide a forum for you to get out there, meet and greet and hand people your business card. You can find a list of the larger shows at www.biztradeshows.com and find details by industry or country. There's also www.eventseye.com, another global listing of events by location, topic or date. Check your local business network websites because they may also list sector specific events and exhibitions. In the UK, www.exhibitions.co.uk has details of fairs and exhibitions. If you're planning to go as an exhibitor, www.businesslink.gov.uk has some first class tips on how to make the most of a show.

Fairs and exhibitions may be specialist in nature, covering a particular sector, or generic. They are not necessarily organised by university careers fairs – local careers companies may also run fairs for the public, at which there will probably be far fewer graduates. The graduate fairs take place all over the country, often with a sector focus, such as the African Caribbean Diversity Fair; finance and management; Engineering Science and IT; Alternatives Fair; Volunteering Fair, and so on. Some are very specific, such as Newcastle University's Annual International Marine Science Careers Fair. Check out the Prospects website at www.prospects.ac.uk and www.iop.org for information about the Institute of Physics, Science, Engineering and Technology Fairs.

Plan for a successful event

When you approach stand-holders, an introductory chat about their company and what it's developing and working on can quickly lead to a sentence or two about yourself and your career goals. Regardless of whether you're going to a trade show or careers event, tips for a successful show include:

- Pre-register online to avoid lengthy queues.
- Identify the people you want to meet and visit their websites *before* you go. On arrival, visit their stands *first* while you're fresh and full of energy.
- Create a business card for yourself to hand out. Put your contact details (email and mobile number) and your most recent or relevant educational qualification on one side with niche areas; and the company you're looking for plus skills you have to contribute on the other.
- Prepare questions to ask before you go to avoid mumbling and stumbling over awkward introductory waffle. *'What advice do you have for someone in my position?'* and *'What job hunting strategies can you suggest I use?'* can be two helpful questions to get insider information and give you other routes to follow.
- Ask open questions. 'Do you recruit graduates of any discipline?' is a closed question requiring a simple 'yes' or 'no' answer; you won't learn much. *'What degrees do you particularly look to recruit?'* is hard to answer with a 'yes' or 'no'. As an open question, it gives you more information and enables you to engage the person you're talking to in further conversation.
- If someone looks busy, wait until they are quieter later.
- Talk to people in the café areas. Make some small talk about the fair – *'Are you here as an exhibitor?'*, *'What does your company do?'*, *'I'll stop by and see you at your stand!'*. Smaller companies may not have a stand, but you might bump into a representative from one if you start talking to people in the café areas.
- When the event is over, reflect over what you've learnt about the opportunities available and yourself. Bring together action points and carry them through. Business cards create dust if unused; you want them to create results.

◆ Write and thank the people you met at the show by email or letter. If you have a web CV, you can attach the address under your contact details at the bottom.

Heading to other shores – working abroad

This may be particularly appropriate if you're thinking, '*Well, my industry is dead in this country. So what now?*'. In this case, you have a couple of choices before you. You can switch to an allied industry, in which your degree may still come in useful, you can change altogether, or you can start your own business. Could you, for example, export anything which is needed by the industry in those regions where it is flourishing?

Ten questions to ask include:

1 What is the local job market like?
2 How do employers recruit staff there? What is involved?
3 How should I write a CV for that country?
4 What organisations and websites can I turn to for advice and information, such as Prospects and Hobsons?
5 Does my professional body have any links in the country I wish to work in? What support can it give me?
6 How will my current qualifications transfer? Will they be accepted? Many professional bodies are working with other countries across borders to ensure the smooth transfer and recognition of qualifications from one nation to another. Is the country I'm going to more interested in experience than a qualification?
7 How does the working environment differ? What is acceptable behaviour and what is not?
8 What level of job would I have with the competences I have?
9 Will I need to take additional tests to prove my competence in my new country before I can start work?
10 Where in the world will my knowledge and skills be needed in the future?

Put '*willing to relocate*' on your CV or business card but be prepared actually to do it. If you're focusing in on one country and you satisfy visa requirements, say so on your CV or covering letter (see www.workpermit.com). Look out for events and newspaper supplements promoting life or companies abroad. Use your network to help you get work overseas. Read journals and newspapers. Make use of embassies and state employment services. The European Job Mobility Portal (http://europa.eu.int/eures) is one of the places where European candidates can see an employer's vacancy and employers can multi-search for CVs which may meet their needs. It links the public employment services in Europe and helps people take up work in other member states of the EEA. It has information on jobs, learning, labour markets, health and registering for work when you arrive, and working conditions. You could also sign up with a recruitment agency that has international offices or connections, or go through an organisation offering placements abroad, such as GAP, or simply do it yourself.

Going home later on

The various locations you choose to work need to be kept in mind when you're considering where to settle later in life. Sooner or later, you may want to come home. Watch for any trends or new laws or regulations there which may impede on your ability to return when the time comes. Consider the financial implications for your future. How will working abroad affect any pension due to you later in life, for example, be it state or private? Read *Working Abroad, The Complete Guide to Overseas Employment* by Jonathan Reuvid (see Further reading).

Your next steps:

1   List employers in the sector you wish to work in to research in the country you want to work in.
2   Develop a short list by researching them through the web, careers fairs, finding out about their products and services, your network, news items.
3   Who do you know, or which sector networks could you tap into, to acquire an introduction to these companies?

Hunting that postgraduate opportunity

We have focused primarily on job hunting in this chapter, but you may, of course, be on the look-out for a postgraduate course. There are a number of websites to help you, such as FindaPhd, FindaMasters, and these are listed in Useful addresses and further information, together with the relevant research councils. It is important that you make an informal visit to meet the team you would be working under, in particular your supervisor if you are thinking of doing a PhD. A postgraduate course is not a move to be taken lightly and you need to consider questions similar to the individual heading into employment to ensure that you are taking the right next step. Tap into all the resources available, and consider questions such as:

- Which institutions offer the subject I wish to study at university? Which appeal and which can I put aside?
- What are my needs in postgraduate study and will each course meet them?
- What are the areas of specialist expertise on offer within each department? How would I be contributing to that?
- What are the facilities like? What research funding does the institution and this department get?
- What reputation does it have?
- What makes up its networks in terms of the employers it works for and with, the research institutes, societies?
- What other (if any) responsibilities will I be expected to take on?
- Does the culture of the department suit me?
- What am I doing to secure funding?
- When is the deadline to apply?
- What will I need to make the application? Who will my referees be? What other tests will I need to sit?

It would be worth meeting with a careers adviser to go through the necessarily steps you will need to take to get a place on a postgraduate course, preferably someone who can help you as you work through your degree.

Moving things forward ... do you, don't you?

Find out more about the organisation and its career opportunities, but don't confine your research to the company's website. Delve further and wider for any mention of it in the local, national or international media. Most employers try to provide as much information as they can about their organisation to job hunters so that the latter can ensure they are applying to the right sort of company for them. Why not see if you can get in touch with someone appropriate at the company to see if you can visit and look round, and talk about the opportunities available?

Ten questions to ask of a company or organisation:

1   What is its mission and what does it want to do and achieve? Does it excite you?
2   What messages does it give you about its values and what it deems to be important? What values does the organisation or company portray in its advertising, literature, image and brand? Look for evidence that it upholds these values. Do they excite you?
3   The size of the organisation and how that will impact on the way people work and the opportunities within it.
4   Where it is located? Is it spread over a number of websites?
5   Its structure and hierarchy; is there just the one company or are there a number of subsidiary companies within one group?
6   How is it organised? A small company may have one person looking after IT, marketing, sales, web design and HR which would put a generalist business degree to excellent use; a large one will have a department of people for each of these elements enabling you to focus on one area.
7   What is the company's financial position? If it is not healthy, your career there may be short. What are its strengths, weaknesses, opportunities and threats?
8   What sort of people work for it? Look at employee profiles. What do they get involved with outside work? How do they describe themselves, the company and their roles?
9   What is the company doing to be innovative and competitive?
10 If you are looking to work for a scientific company, find out what research and development it is working on at the moment. Do these projects excite you?

Eight key questions to ask yourself:

1   What could you contribute to this organisation in terms of skills and qualities?
2   Is this the sort of place you'd look forward to walking into every Monday morning?
3   Could you see yourself working for them in five years' time?
4   Can they offer you the future you're looking for?

5   What would you need to do to make the career progress you want to enjoy? What support would you get from the company?

6   How could you secure a foot in the door?

7   Is there a vacancy right now you could apply for or will you need to make contact on spec?

8   What actions are you going to take next and when?

You could multiply the opportunities before you if you consider working for an organisation in the short term, perhaps on a contract basis or freelance basis to get your foot in the door. Part-time work will leave you free to job hunt for the role you really want, or to develop your own business while bringing some money in. A small company may not have enough work to warrant taking someone on full time but it may offer you freelance work. Think laterally and creatively when you're job hunting.

Starting your own business

There is more help around than ever before for those with an entrepreneurial spirit but still too many start-ups fail for lack of sufficient advice and research. The BusinessLink network in England helps small companies and start-ups. Visit www.businesslink.gov.uk to find your local link. There's information on setting up a business, writing a business plan, accessing funding, growing your business and even selling it on. There are also links to the sister organisations in Scotland, Wales and Northern Ireland.

Consider initiatives

Aside from the National Council for Graduate Entrepreneurship (see page 42), other national examples of organisations helping people to set up on their own include Shell LiveWIRE, the Prince's Trust, Start-ups and the Prime Initiative for the over fifties (see Useful Addresses and Further Information). Some initiatives may be national in nature, others very local. The National Endowment for Science, Technology and the Arts may also have schemes to support graduates who wish to build new companies. Visit www.nesta.org.uk for more information.

Eight questions to consider are:

1   What's your vision? What do you want to achieve with this business?
2   What are your products and services?
3   What to you need to get up and running, such as:
    • somewhere to work from
    • equipment needed to set up (you may have a lot of this already)
    • computer/lap top/ipod
    • communications – internet, phone, fax
    • marketing and publicity materials – possibly a website, business cards, brochures, membership of professional and business networks
    • insurance, professional indemnity and public liability;
    • training
    • a salary/wage.
4   Who can support you?
5   What new skills and knowledge will you need?
6   Who are your competitors?
7   What research do you need to do?
8   Where will you get funding from?

Summary action points

Move your thinking further forward:

1   What are agencies in the region doing to encourage businesses to take on graduates, particular those in my sector?
2   How much do I know about the work I want to do and how to get 'in' to it?
3   Where are most of the employers located in this sector?
4   Which other areas are showing a rapid growth?
5   What am I doing to enjoy life and have time out while I'm working towards my goals?

Chapter 6

Proving yourself

From scholar to worker

One minute you're a student and the next you're not. You may choose to have some time out or get going on your career straight away, but whichever path you take, there's a big difference between the two. The earlier you start preparing for life after your university days, including postgraduate work, the easier it will be to settle in work and life afterwards.

Making the psychological switch

It's time to leave some habits behind and start behaving differently. You've probably had a fantastic time, and learnt a great deal, but if you were a full-time student, it's time to take stock and recognise that the fun days – and yes, we know you worked hard – are behind you and its time to move on. You may be feeling a keen sense of loss, a wonderment of what comes next, a sure certainty that the world's your oyster and the wealth of opportunities out there, but how on earth will any of it relate to you back home?

There is quite a switch from being a student to becoming an employee or researcher, because the impact of your work and how well you do it affects other people, as Table 6.1 shows.

The 'learning to do' referred to above relates to those things you cannot be taught until you start work, such as product knowledge specific to the organisation you join. But at the very least, employers want to know that you know how to behave at work and that you understand what work is like.

At work, you'll still get the person who does it all the last minute, those who are indecisive, bullies, patronising or negative, who spout 'We've always done it like this' and see no reason to change. There are the moody and lazy, working alongside power-crazy, highly competitive workaholics, and you'll need to deal with

Table 6.1

As a student		As an employee
Studying	*and*	Working
Being a student	*and*	An employee/employer
Learning	*and*	Doing or learning to do ...
Student responsibilities	*and*	Responsibilities at work towards: team; clients, customers; company/employer; your own colleagues, peers
The hours you choose to work	*and*	The hours you're expected to work
Holidays	*and*	Average four weeks holiday – in the USA, probably one or two weeks in the first few years
The way you dress and behave	*and*	The image and behaviour that's right and appropriate for work
Long-term personal goals	*and*	Vision, mission, targets need the goodwill and motivation of everyone on board
Rules and regulations in your university	*and*	Employment laws, health and safety, professional regulations
Meeting deadlines – it's just you that suffers	*and*	Meeting deadlines – other people are depending on you
The pace of life – you can dictate it	*and*	The pace of work is dictated by the industry and demands of clients and customers. Your day can change dramatically on receipt of a phone call. People expect fast responses. Are you adaptable and flexible?
Your performance – it affects just you	*and*	Your performance can affect that of your team and the company – it can clinch a deal, save the company money
You can control pretty much most things in your life	*and*	There are many things you can control but equally there are many you cannot

them all. Your skills and talents in motivating and managing people will be well tested as you progress and work to bring out the best in your team. You'll need your influencing and persuading skills to encourage those around you to see the benefits of what you want to do. But your experiences at university will have given you a good start in speaking up for yourself and getting along with people from all different backgrounds and with their own aspirations. Add work experience in a real live work situation, and you can put the above skills into place and make the psychological switch.

Transferable skills are essential to enjoy life and excel at work

List everything you'd done during your university days and you'd be astonished at what you've achieved formally and informally. To do it all, you'll have used skills which transfer from one aspect of life to another, such as communication. To communicate effectively with clients and colleagues, family and friends, you need to express yourself clearly orally and in writing through email, letter and fax. You need to be able to empathise with and understand the needs of others.

Rank the transferable skills in Figure 6.1 in order of your strength, 5 being the strongest.

Now find evidence for each one looking through your list of extra-curricular activities, voluntary efforts, work experience, academic work. Which are your strengths? Which are your weaknesses and how are you tackling them? Take each transferable skill and give an example of a time when you've used it. Consider all the angles you might be asked about it.

Have you made the most of university life?

University days offer the chance to create a life out of a blank canvas. Employers will be looking to see how you occupied your time and what you learnt from your activities. They'll be looking for evidence of your passion for your subject, such as shows you've been to, and competitions you've entered, any writing you've done in your spare time (if appropriate)? What projects have you done over and above your coursework which might be of interest to potential employers or clients and customers? What modes of learning did you use which could transfer over to the workplace, such as giving presentations,

	5	4	3	2	1
1 Organising/planning					
2 Communicating, orally					
3 Communicating, written					
4 Learning					
5 Creativity					
6 Decision making					
7 Self-motivation					
8 Strategic planning					
9 Handling change					
10 Problem solving					
11 Team working					
12 Leadership					
13 Adaptability, flexibility					
14 Self-awareness					
15 Commercial awareness					

Figure 6.1

undertaking research, debating a point in seminars and tutorials, critiquing your work, taking an idea from conception to fruition, working in a team to solve a problem?

Effectiveness and high performance at work is built on the right attitude, a professional competence and approach, product and sector knowledge, a *drive* to make things happen and soft skills. At university, you develop skills through various academic and extra-curricular activities. To progress your career, you need continued exposure to different experiences and the right training and personal development, all of which continue to expand your capabilities, push back your comfort zones and build on your soft or transferable skills. Self-awareness, self-promotion and self-presentation also count, along with keeping abreast of career developments and news in your field. Figure 6.2 below shows how university and work link together incorporating all these elements.

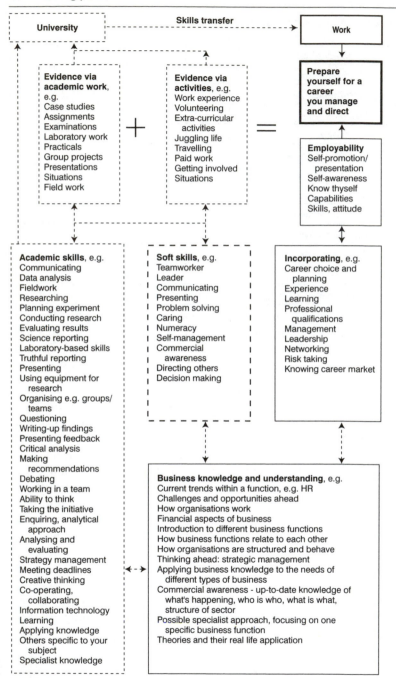

Figure 6.2

This extends beyond work!

Throughout your life, both in and out of work, you'll need to manage a number of ingredients, as Table 6.2 shows.

Who are you?

This is not just about your qualifications and experience to date. They certainly contribute and play a part, but this is more about how you arrived at the whole-rounded individual you are now. It's not about '*Well, I completed my UCAS form and made my six choices, and then sat and prayed that I'd get in to my first choice!*'. It's about, how did you come to apply at all? What and who moulded your decisions and what did you need *within yourself* to get to where you are today? What resources did you pull out of your body, heart, mind and soul to make your degree happen and how can you build on them and use them to maximum effect throughout your life? Who did you work alongside as you strove to achieve your mutual goals? (*That's teamwork!*)

It's also about your values, and what matters to you. After all, you must have chosen the path you took for a reason. So what lies behind and within you, what makes you tick, what drives, inspires and motivates you? What challenges and dramas have you faced? How have you tackled them? (*That's problem solving.*) If you wrote your life story, what particular achievements would you want your readers to know about? What journeys would you want to tell them about? How can you show them that you've turned your plans into action? Have you done a stint of travelling, or juggled study and work at the same time? (*Shows adaptability and flexibility, planning and organisation.*) When have you really had to knuckle down and make things happen? Were there times when you kept going when everything else seems to be going against you? How many times have you failed in something – anything – and you've tried and tried

Table 6.2

Yourself	Information technology
People	Resources
Teams	Materials
Time	Projects
Money	Deadlines
Your energy	Research
The client's expectations	The facilities around you
Your future	Your suppliers

again until success came your way? (*Persistence, motivation, drive, resilience.*) What changes have you dealt with in your life? If you've driven them yourself how have you tapped into your drive and energy and passion to make them happen? If they happened outside your control, how did you handle them? (*Resilience, ability to ride through change.*) What negative experiences have you been through that you've learnt from? How could you show a stranger the person you truly are, as opposed to a bunch of qualifications listed neatly on a page? (*That's written communication, persuading, influencing, expressing.*) What sort of person would they see? It's these qualities that you need to bring out in your CV or interviews when applying for jobs or courses. (*That's self-promotion.*)

It's also about those things which prompted you to make the choices you have in work, play and leisure, in your friends you hang around with. (*That shows what motivates you.*) What circumstances have you grown up in which have influenced you, your actions, your choices and the messages you've taken on board about yourself, life, the opportunities ahead? (*Decision making and action planning skills here.*) What have you done to challenge them? (*You don't settle for just anything!*) What have you done to help yourself? These sorts of things have all contributed to make up the person you are by influencing and moulding you over the years. It will also show you that being successful – however you define success – takes tremendous hard graft, self-discipline and continual, sustained effort. Without ingredients such as these, success all too often feels hollow, empty and unsatisfying. Look at all the times you've been proactive and what the results were. Look at the opportunities you created for yourself by getting off your backside and making something happen. (*Taking the initiative.*) If you want to be successful in the way you envisage success, you need to do that again and again.

However you've studied towards your degree, be it full-time, part-time or by distance learning, congratulate yourself. Go out with a group of friends and sink a few drinks. But take time quietly, independently and proudly to assess what you've achieved and, crucially, the characteristics in your personality, the motivators and drivers which have empowered you to success, such as persistence, determination and curiosity. You've had the endurance to get through a degree, and developed the ability to network, to form working relationships fast, to take responsibility for your own career development and learning and to be resourceful.

Acknowledge your strengths and resources in writing

Written down, they will give you a lift, especially if you're feeling low. Whatever stage of life you're at, you'll need to draw on all your resources to create the future you want. Get ready to dig deep and raise your energy levels, standards, focus, persistence and drive to a higher level to propel yourself into making it happen. Finally, you'll be able to tell employers more succinctly what lies behind the person you are – and the person you want to be, thereby selling yourself more effectively. Self-presentation and promotion is an important skill at work today.

Make the most of programmes on offer to help postgraduates

In the UK, an example is the UK GRAD programme to support the academic sector to embed personal and professional skills development into research degree programmes. Visit www.crac. org.uk/insight/gradschools/grad.htm for more information. There will be others. The Science and Innovation Investment Framework 2004–15 lays out the government's plans to increase investment in the core fund of universities and put more money into research, all part of a drive to boost the country's competitiveness. Other countries are doing the same. Look to find out what impact that has for opportunities for you as a graduate.

The power of work experience

Relevant, targeted work experience is becoming more important in the journey to acquire the career you want; indeed, for many careers it is essential. It strengthens your hand in the employment market. Employers can see you in action for themselves: the way you walk and talk, think and act, behave and motivate, initiate and inspire, work and apply your new found knowledge. They want to see how effective you are and how you achieve results. In fact, employers rate work experience and internships as a highly effectively way to find graduate recruits. There are many schemes on offer throughout the year for varying periods of time. Their entry is often highly competitive, requiring the same professional approach and strategy to achieve success as job hunting.

The SME market in its own right can give you the chance to put your foot in the door. There may be a scheme running in your area to help companies and graduates benefit each other. The National Council for Work Experience has a lot more information on its website www.work-experience.org. Also look for opportunities to gain experience through professional bodies and trade associations' websites. Check out www.step.org.uk which arranges placements with companies for a year or shorter periods of time. Many of the websites listed in this book have details of work placements, internships and residencies and you need to get to know which websites are most suitable for you. Internships, residencies and work experience placements are very competitive and it can be hard to do three months with just your travel expenses; but it is an excellent way in, so consider them as an investment, just as your university studies are.

You don't have to sign up for a specific scheme. You could approach a company directly for experience, which may be a great way to get into a smaller company that may not be aware of opportunities to join placement schemes. Keep trying and persisting.

1   Identify what it is that you need to practice at work – are there particular skills you want to use? Pinpoint what you will bring to the employer – enthusiasm and a passion for what you're doing are a start.

2   Give the employer examples of what you can do and what you would like to do, so that he has a menu of choices; as a scientist, have you considered how your laboratory and/or research *skills* may be of help to an employer in an unrelated area, and how you can market them to those who do require your scientific skills?

3   Show him what you have done so far, so that he has a clear idea of what you're capable of. Do you have your scientific knowledge and skills at the tip of your fingers, particularly that relating to the post (academic or business) you want, or could you do with a brush up?

4   Give an allotted timescale but be flexible. Remember that small employers recruit all the year round, for example, whereas large graduate employers' graduate training programmes have deadlines.

5   Find out if the company has a project which needs to be done which no one else has time to do. Offer up your expertise as

a scientist to find out what it is really like to be part of a team
of researchers.

6   Ask for an assessment of your work at the end, so that the
employer can write a testimonial and you can together work
out what you have achieved and got out of the placement.

---

*Think about projects you've done which will be relevant to potential
employers, including those you're looking to do work experience
with.*

Make sure you're ready to talk to interviewers and those on the
look-out for potential recruits about projects and research you've
undertaken:

+ What did you do to make them happen on your own and in
a group?
+ What was the scale of the research or project?
+ How did you approach it?
+ What was the cost?
+ What applications did you use? How did you do your research?
How did you handle the ethics of it and the management of
the project and did you collaborate with anyone else?
+ Be ready to talk technical, especially if you are applying for a
position where your degree/subject knowledge is relevant to
the proposed work in hand.

Work experience should play a central role in your sales strategy
when you start job hunting – it shows you know what you're letting
yourself in for. You can talk about your experiences and achievements
at interview and demonstrate your effectiveness through job-specific
and transferable skills you've used. You can prove how you can be
relied on to get results, your passion for and belief in what you're
doing, your willingness to get your hands dirty; talk the lingo,
understand the frustrations, challenges, issues, opportunities and
threats. And the longer and more relevant the experience, the more
beneficial it will be. And remember, you don't have to take part in
a structured work experience programme – you can find some on
your own.

You can pick up the language relevant to the sector and the
organisation or company itself. You can pick up business lingo
relevant to the business world with terms such as 'profit and loss',

'added value', 'key performance indicators', and you'll understand what they are. Listening skills are important if you're to pick up the language and way of working specific to the business. Each one has its own terminology relating to its systems, protocol, meetings, hierarchy, and many have their own intranet. Work experience gives you insight into how companies function from the small to the large – even working at the bottom of the organisation is a way great to learn how the various parts work, who the key decision-makers are and why the bottom line is so important. It also helps you make those all-important contacts. *'I've got a friend who works in PR. Shall I mention you to her? She could give you a call for a chat'*.

Work to close any skills gaps

Every industry has its problems recruiting staff with the right skills. In many niche areas, there are cluster groups, forums and groups of employers, industry specialists and training providers who are trying to tackle the problem and encourage employers to offer (graduates) a way in and a structured learning environment. Ideas which are being developed include apprenticeship programmes, business realisation schemes, training programmes and career-entry initiatives. Go to the heart of the industry to find out what is being undertaken in yours.

Show someone who works in the sector a copy of your CV; can they spot any skill gaps? If so, how will you close them? A short training programme or perhaps a stint of work experience with exposure to a particular area may help.

So what behaviours and practices do you need to elicit to make your 'it' happen?

Be very determined. Push for your corner, but remain polite. Be ready to sacrifice something else in your life so that you can give what you *really* want the energy and attention hours it deserves.

Immerse yourself in the field you want to be in

Go out there and start building up your experience in any skills you wish to use at work or in your own business.

Start acquiring clients and earning money for the skills you have. For example, many scientific recruitment agencies offer temporary positions or contract work, ideal for the holidays. Write a clear career goal you have at the top of your CV in a short sentence, such as '*Seeking post as a laboratory technician with a company specialising in ... research*'.

If you're job hunting, devote full-time effort to the task. Keep your ambitions at the forefront of your mind night and day, or they will lose their prominence in your heart and it will take more effort to make them happen, especially if you are in a 'lower level' role right now. Position yourself to get out of it, either by moving or staying put, or one of two things can happen, as Figure 6.3 shows.

Network, network, network

Take the wheel of networking in Figure 6.4. At some time in your life, you may focus on one segment more than others; you may want to add or delete a segment. Aim for a balanced wheel, so that you can tap into the support you need for a healthy, balanced life and successful, happy career. Tap into every corner to see if any (albeit unexpectedly) can provide you with the opportunity you need to truly kick off your career and life in the direction you want it to go.

1   What are you doing to make something happen in each segment to create the career and life you want?

2   Which do you need to focus *more* on to get the results you need and make the connections you want?

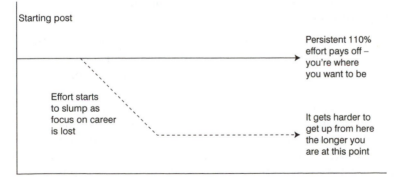

Figure 6.3

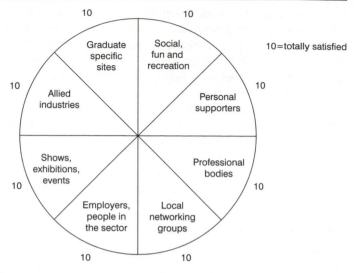

Figure 6.4

3   Which section(s) should the *hub* of your network be at right now so that you can tackle the most important and urgent issues in your life?

4   How much activity do you have in it or them at the moment? How often are you making new contacts? Which methods are yielding the best results?

5   What do you need to do to make sure the sector you need to have the strongest network in is up to par to get the results you need in your life?

Short-term solutions to long-term challenges

Like work experience, temping gives you the opportunity to show what you can do and will often lead to a permanent role.

Five steps to getting 'in' to a company through temping:

1   Hook up with a specialist agency which focuses on the specific sector you want to work in. If you're unsure, go for a high-street name with a graduates division. Visit to the company's website to assess its strengths and focus and track record.

2   When you sign up with an agency, dress as if you're going for an interview so that the agency knows it can send you

out with confidence. Your consultant should talk through your skills, competencies and career goals. Ask how often and by what method you should keep in touch. Check emails and mobile regularly for messages. Try to get two or three week or month assignments together in one sector to enhance your CV's consistency.

3   Reflect weekly on skills and knowledge you're acquiring. Which environments have you thrived most in? What have you achieved? Get feedback from your agency and the company you're with.

4   Update your CV regularly and make sure the agency has the most recent copy.

5   Consider what you need to start doing to make the overall experience more effective and to take you closer to achieving your goals. What strategies can you employ to make these happen?

Many people find work exhausting enough without also doing career planning back home. But this is where 110 per cent commitment and effort will get you to where you want to be, while the 90 per cent won't, so raise your standard.

How do you take time out to go for interviews?

Companies are paying for you to be there and do the job they need you to do, not to keep disappearing for interviews with others. Keep calling in sick, and you look unreliable in the eyes of the agency *and* employer. Can you interview first thing in the morning or late afternoon, or work extra hours the day before or after any interview? Give your temporary employer as much notice as possible. Work at 110 per cent and they won't want to lose you. Ask your agency for advice in handling the situation.

Don't wait for doors to open for you. Get out there and start knocking on doors to connect to the opportunities you want while you're working or studying.

Learn from others you deem to be successful. How do they do it?

Seek out those who are where you wish to be. They've done it. But *how did they get there?* People love to talk about themselves and many will see it as a compliment if you ask their advice. If they see passion and enthusiasm in you, they'll be more than happy to help.

So go to careers shows, conferences, relevant trade shows and exhibitions and talk to people. Be friendly and interested. How did people get to where they are today? What advice would they have for you? What has their career path been and what are the three most important factors which have contributed to their success? Contact people you deem successful. What lessons they have learnt along the way that they can pass on to you? Read Sarah Brown's book, *Moving on up*, with advice and stories from leaders in many sectors on how they got to the top and what it takes. If you want to be a postgraduate, ask one in your department if you can meet up and talk to them about their life and how their day differs to those undergraduate years. What advice would they have for you?

Get ahead: get a mentor

Mentors have been there, done it and got the t-shirt. They can be an invaluable source of help, advice and contacts. A mentor will talk to you about your goals, aspirations and how you can get there. They will help you stay on track and keep focused. There are lots of mentor programmes available though many specialist networking groups and you should look at various websites listed throughout this book to find one which suits your needs. Mentoring can be done face-to-face or over the telephone.

Heading for self-employment?

Consider these questions:

- Name three companies which are success stories. They can be any size.
- What makes them successful?
- What works well for them? What doesn't?
- What makes customers and clients turn to them for products and services?

* What can you learn from them and apply to your own business?

Now let's do this exercise differently:

* Name three companies which have not been successful or which are going through a really rough time.
* Where are they going wrong?
* What are they trying to do to put things right?
* What has put customers and clients off them for products and services?
* What can you learn from them and apply to your own business?

Brainstorm with friends or join forces with other graduates to see what you can learn from them and their outlook.

Summary action points

Turn your experience from an academic one into a work-related one which means something to employers and gets you in the right mind-set.

1   Look to see how you can start living the working day so far as possible.
2   Identify steps you can take which will bring you closer to the role you want.
3   Review your progress to date in terms of your own self-awareness; your picture of your career and life in the next three to five years; how your network has changed; and what you've done in relation to taking your next step.
4   How can you change your behaviour to get the success you want? What could you do differently?

Chapter 7

Promoting yourself

The next stage, as you prepare to sell yourself, is to consider questions such as:

- What is most relevant in your life history for you to tell recruiters about when you consider the opportunities you seek?
- What can you control, such as the amount of time you spend researching a company prior to an interview, the way you present yourself and the time you spend considering what you can contribute to the company?
- What can you not do anything about (such as the numbers of applicants going for a particular job)?

Turn your skills and talents into a marketable commodity. Promote the skills you need to get the work.

A degree in biological sciences opens the door to many careers, but you need to look at the job you are applying for and consider the range of skills and knowledge the employer is looking for. For example, if you're applying for a role in which your science skills will simply *complement* your work, the employer will want to know about the other skills you have and may consider your scientific knowledge to be a bonus. If your science abilities are essential to the job in hand, then you *will* need put more emphasis on your science abilities, but also emphasise skills such as working to deadlines, time management, accuracy and lab skills. Make your CV and application as relevant as you can to the employer who will be reading it. Postgraduate students will need to be particularly adept at selling the skills and qualities you have acquired as a result of your extra qualification, such as self-direction, resilience and initiative.

If you're applying for work abroad, find out how employers recruit in that country and what they look for in an application.

Some won't be interested in your hobbies and interests, whereas others will, so learn about the job hunting culture in the country you wish to work in and adopt it in your application.

Remember, enlist several ways of job hunting – don't put all your eggs into one basket. Aim to do something with each method at least once a week.

Once you've identified a vacancy, course or employer you want to go for:

1   Identify any deadlines so that you can work out what to do when, and pinpoint what needs to be done.
2   Assess the skills, knowledge, acumen and attitude your potential employer needs by researching their organisation carefully.
3   Identify the evidence you need to paint the picture of your capabilities and aspirations from your research, life resources, characteristics to date, work experience, voluntary work, travel, leisure, team efforts and projects.
4   If you need to send a CV in, write it out until you are comfortable with it; produce a one-page letter of application and anything else required. In your one-page letter, highlight the skills and experience you have which are relevant to the role you're applying for, and explain why the company you're writing to appeals to you. Show you know something about the company by mentioning a campaign they have been involved with; for example, a project they have worked on, or some news you discovered in the press about their work.
5   Before you send your application in, get someone to check a printed version for you. Copy it, so that you can refer to it before interview.

To save time, understand how companies recruit

If you're applying to a small company (50 people or less), you may simply need to send a carefully thought through and well presented letter of application and your CV to the boss – you can find out who that is from the company's website. Spell out what your qualifications mean to make life easy for them – leave out educational jargon. Large corporates, however, may want applicants to complete an online or paper application form, or do an online psychometric test or personality questionnaire. Many employers run initial screening through short telephone interviews with candidates, followed by assessment centres, interviews and more. A graduate recruitment section will probably lead the process.

If you have to complete an application form, and send a CV with it, it is tempting to put 'See CV' in answer to many questions. Such lack of effort will inevitably lead to your application being binned. Application forms give recruiters an opportunity to compare applicants, so apply the 110 per cent effort rule as opposed to 80 per cent.

Put in an outstanding application, not just an excellent one

In the recruitment process, there is one winner, i.e. the person who is selected, who will stand out over the other applicants and be the right fit with the team. The person who is selected will have probably given an outstanding performance from start to finish; the others may all be excellent, but in a competitive world, there is only one winner. So if you're going to put yourself a cut above all the other applicants, you need to make yourself stand out as an outstanding candidate.

Get physical

It's a competitive world out there; prepare yourself to fight for your part in it. Exercise daily to sharpen your mind and body, boost your energy and focus. Minimise the rubbish you eat and drink, including alcohol. Mental agility exercises will help you improve your ability to think on your feet.

Put yourself in the recruiters' shoes

Think about what you know about the company and the sector, and the role they are recruiting for. What are they after? What do they want? One retail recruiter offering retail management training programmes wants: *'Customer service – it's vital for us. They need to be able to relate to the general public and to the staff who they'll be responsible for. We need to see that in a CV'.* A company looking for a lab researcher may demand a particular degree, or research skills, or want a particular level of technical knowledge. Another employer may refer to particular skills which are essential to the job. Look for clues as to what the employer is after.

Get practice in tests and read up on the recruitment process

If you know tests will form part of the assessment, do a practice run in your university careers service. Get used to handling questions, managing your time, and focusing on a task. The website www. prospects.ac.uk enables you to get your CV checked and talk to graduate employers and practice online personality and aptitude tests so that you know what you are letting yourself in for.

There are plenty of specialist books regarding CVs, application forms, applying online, assessment centres and the interview process, and these are all listed in Useful addresses and further information. Raise your standard over all the other candidates: invest a few hours in a good read. Look for tips from agencies' websites on the application process and follow them.

Five golden rules to kick off, whether you are applying for a job or postgraduate course or position:

1   Use a professional email address, putting your contact details at the bottom and an appropriate header in the subject box. Address it to the right person; check their name on the company's website or by calling the switchboard.

2   Check your mobile and email regularly for messages. Recruitment can move quickly.

3   Make your application easy to read with bullet points, not prose. Explain your educational qualifications – spell out subjects you covered and the skills you've acquired.

4   On your CV, use a short opening statement or sentence to describe your career aims or at least the role you are looking for. Describe the person who lies behind the CV or application form through your use of adjectives.

5   Be accurate with grammar and spelling. Ensure your application shows off your ability to express yourself well.

Make CVs personal and relevant to the company, organisation or institute you're writing to.

If the role you're after is a scientific/research-based one, include a section outlining your scientific skills and knowledge. And if you've had work experience or employment, include a few words about the company's speciality, size and location so that the reader can instantly build a picture of how your role fitted in. Publications – include any scientific papers or articles you've written, including where they were published, and also those in progress. Include any research projects you've undertaken and pinpoint the skills you used. Think about what the employer needs and show him or her that you have it, be it relevant lab skills or capabilities in writing and undertaking surveys. Make the link between what you have and what the employer is after.

A CV should include headings for areas such as:

- Contact details (at the very top, easily spotted).
- Academic history (most recent first), pinpointing the most relevant aspects of your course to the employer and mentioning any exemptions from professional qualifications the course has given you, if relevant. Include the skills you have acquired during your course.
- As mentioned above, papers you may have published or research projects you have worked on – don't to forget to expand on research and laboratory skills where relevant.
- Work experience, which outlines projects you have worked on, and gives an idea of the size of each company you have worked for.
- Overall achievements and positions of responsibility.
- Personal details – for example, *'Willing to relocate'* if you are; a clean driving licence; marital status and age (put date of birth as opposed to age in years).
- Interests and leisure – keep it brief and honest.

Pay particular attention to the way you lay out your CV, from the font size and type to the layout and way you organise the information you wish to portray. Keep it simple, but make it look good. Limit it to two sides of A4 paper or less, one page if you're doing it online. Send it by email or on paper (good quality white A4 with no gimmicks, designs, wrinkles or coffee stains). Consider the sector you want to work in. Some – such as the professions – accountancy, banking, law, etc. – expect conventional CVs. Others such as the media expect candidates to be more creative with attention to layout and typescript, but not pretentious.

Are you heading for any of the following?		Obtain evidence of your:
		• Passions and interests
• Employment		• Values and motivation
• Work experience		• Ability to contribute to
• Internship	*To sell yourself succesfully,*	their success
• Further study	*you will need to show that*	• Skills: transferable and
• Initiatives such as Knowledge	*you've got what they need*	job-specific
Transfer Partnerships		• Experience
• Postgraduate course		• Technical expertise
• Short training course		• Research skills
		(if appropriate)
		• Laboratory skills (if
		appropriate)
		• An understanding of
		what it's like to be at
		work or in academia
		• Something that grabs
		their attention and makes
		you stand out
		• Level of relevant
		knowledge

Figure 7.1

Many applications are riddled with spelling errors, hard to read and poorly researched. They get deleted. Others get a glance and perhaps go into a 'think about while reading the rest' pile. Some are easy to read and relevant, and then one or two will make the employer think *'There's that one line which makes me sit up and think, wow – I've just got to meet this person'.*

Figure 7.1 shows some of the features you need to think about.

They want one year's experience

If you were to add up all your work experience and put it together on your CV, you may be surprised to find that it adds up to close to a year. Can you add to that paid and unpaid experience, commissions, contracts, work simulated projects, voluntary efforts? Put all your work experience together in a CV and put it first before your educational qualifications so that it draws the employer's attention before anything else. Similarly, if the organisation wants someone with a particular qualification, but you feel as though you really do have relevant experience and that the job is right for you, why not call up to find out how vital that qualification truly is?

If the job really appeals but you're missing one or two things that they ask for, call up to see if it is still worth you applying.

Consider the skills and qualities success a recruiter wants, be it for a job or course or research. For example, have you:

* Worked with a team to a tight deadline?
* Collaborated with people on a piece of research?
* Managed a team of people?
* Initiated projects or activities – created your own project, worked out the research which needs to be done and managed the process from idea to end result?
* Taken responsibility?
* Showed resourcefulness?
* Showed flexibility and adaptability?
* Debated a point with someone and influenced them, and stood your ground making presentations against people who have argued against your findings?
* Taken responsibility for your own learning and career development?
* Been driven to achieve results such as uncovering the answer to a question you wanted to answer?
* Showed you can work across cultures – important if you're going to collaborate with scientists of all different nationalities, for example?

Some of these may be more important to one recruiter than others. In a scientific role, an employer may particularly look for evidence that you can show attention to detail, that you are capable of thinking independently, that you can meet deadlines, follow instructions, that you're meticulous and that you are pig-headed and won't give up!

Outline relevant work and projects to date

Paint a picture of the scale of any relevant projects you've worked on, with information on its size, who it was for, what it was about, numbers, targets, deadlines, results, feedback, percentages and so on. Choose the most relevant to the role you want. If relevant, describe any research you've done, together with any awards you've won, and articles you've written. If your degree grants you exemptions to certain professional qualifications, say so. Be specific about the technology and computer applications you can use.

Look at your potential: where do you want to be?

Where do you see yourself in five years' time? Who *do you want to become?* Increasingly, job prospects relate to the person you are and want to become (your potential), hence the heavy emphasis on psychological tests, assessment centres and even handwriting analysis in the recruitment process. It is not a good idea to say *'I'd like to be running my own company'* or *'I'll be travelling on a year off'* or *'I'd like to be in your job'.* Show ambition, but not at the expense of the interviewer, unless you're applying for a large company where there are clear ladders of progression. An employer will also want to know that you're a stayer. The recruitment process is a long and costly one, so they won't want to take on somebody who intends to leave within a year plus of joining, unless you move up their ranks.

This is a question that employers like to ask when recruiting and many job hunters think, *'Wow. I don't even know where I want to be next week! Why are these guys so hooked on this question?'.* The thing is, recruiting and training staff costs money and time and it's a risk. Employers need to know where your level of ambitions and drive are taking you, what your values and aspirations are and where you see yourself going. They need to look at the staff they are recruiting, to assess the spread of talents and skills they need, and how you might fit and contribute to fulfilling their long-term vision, now and in the future. Large global organisations, for example, may have had to forecast their recruitment needs over a year ago. But many companies also recruit as the need arises, particularly if they are small, asking *'What could this person do for us starting from Monday?'* on the one hand, and wanting people who can grow with and contribute to the organisation on the other.

The fact that you have a degree shows your commitment to learning and developing yourself and realising your potential. An employer can see that by evidence of your conscious decision to study for a degree. They know you have the ability to learn and juggle life, study and work and progress. They can build on your strengths, weaknesses, skills, creativity, leadership abilities and management material. They can train you, probably promote you, give you a team of people to manage and expect results from you. They may provide financial and timely support for you to study towards professional examinations but they need to know that you can and will stand the pace of working relatively long hours during the weekday and studying at night. They'll look for the evidence in your application from start to finish.

More importantly, any potential employer and you need to know that you're right for each other. This is very much a two-way process. If you are not right for each other, it's far better to acknowledge it immediately. The way the organisation is structured may not enable you to meet your aspirations. Equally, if you're going on to further study, make sure you and the thing you are applying for, be it a course or role, are right for you and your long-term plans.

Interestingly, this also applies if you want to set up your own business – know where you are and where you're going, and you're more likely to get there.

Postgraduate? Consider the difference ...

If you've been immersed in research.for several years, it can be hard to pinpoint your transferable skills. Stand back and ask yourself: what has changed about you and your approach as a result of your postgraduate studies? What particular skills, knowledge and breadth have you acquired from them and how would that make a difference to an employer? What difference has it made to your character and personality, your strength, direction and self-belief? How can you show employers that you have extra fine tuned skills in analytical thinking, communication, self-management, motivation and the way you look at how things are done and how other people think, work and do things? How can you avoid employers treating you as if you were an undergraduate when you know there is a difference? How has your level of thinking changed? If you are finding it difficult to identify your transferable skills, book an appointment with a careers adviser and ask them to help you. And don't forget to look at your life overall and look for evidence of your transferable skills in activities such as voluntary work, extra-curricular activities, involvement in committees, clubs and societies. They all add up and count. Be clear about what you have achieved in your studies, as well as considering the journey to whatever result you acquired (as in your findings).

It is worth doing some research of your own into what it is exactly that employers love about PhD students, particularly those who actively seek to recruit them. Such a process could broaden your view of what you have to offer. Your in-depth thinking, analysing, searching for answers, questioning systematic researching approach will undoubtedly help.

Prepare to show your commercial awareness

For instance, if you are seeking a position in a lab in the commercial world, you will need to show that you know your sector: the industry news, the movers and shakers, the main players. Where does the company fit into the sector and how does it stand out from its competitors? Why does it appeal to you over them? Can you talk about its products and services, culture and ethos? How have they grown? You want to join a company which is on the up, not one which is spluttering and faltering. Who are their main clients or customers and what have their recent campaigns, products and services been? Which other organisations and companies have specialists working on similar projects? What are the hot issues of the day? Who is in the headlines and why? Check share prices and read recent annual reports to see how far the company is moving towards achieving its goals or vision. Research the company through the internet and printed press, and talk to people who know about it. Your one-page covering letter of application can make a good start in showing this off as you outline why you chose the company to apply to over its competitors. If you're applying for a voluntary or public organisation, show again that you understand how it is positioned alongside other groups. Another key thing you may want to display is your understanding of how working in research in industry differs from doing so in the academic world.

Show how you can benefit the company and fit in

Demonstrate that you have researched these points:

- What is the company's mission and vision?
- How does it expect to achieve that? What will it need to achieve it?
- What sort of drive and personal qualities from its employees will it need to be successful?
- What can you contribute to the organisation as works to achieve its vision?
- What does the consumer/client want?
- What are the trends and challenges facing the sector?
- What qualities will they be looking for in their employees? How can you demonstrate that you have them?

- What research projects are they working on now? How does the position you are applying for relate to them? How does your background relate to that research?
- What specific job skills does the recruiter call for that you can prove you have?
- What can you bring to the team that might be an added dimension?
- Are you ready to answer competency-based questions, giving employers a clear picture of how you approach problems and processes?
- Can you show that if they sponsor you for a professional qualification or a postgraduate course, you have the staying power to see it through?

Each boss or line-manager has their own criteria to meet as they recruit for a role. These may refer to particular skills which are essential to the job, such as particular IT packages, and will assess every application throughout against this criteria; they may ask the same questions of all candidates to compare their answers. Your prospective boss will look at your skills set and how they will fit with his requirements and, crucially, how you will fit in with the team.

What happens after sending your application in?

Ask your housemates to answer the phone with courtesy, in case a potential employer is calling you. Keep your details, pen and paper and CV by the phone, so you can quickly refer to grades you've had if asked or pull information required.

Go into the recruitment process prepared to have fun

Most recruiters want to give you a good experience – they know you'll tell friends and family what you thought of them. They know that if you are not in a situation where you can be yourself, they won't see the true you. At the end of the day, recruiters have a responsibility to take the right people on for the right roles – no easy task. Be prepared for the interviewer whose technique is appalling –

rambling, non-stop, rude and arrogant. The website www.doctorjob.com can tell you more.

Attending an interview

Dress the part

Review your appearance.

- Polish your shoes and get them re-heeled
- Clean your nails
- Get a hair cut
- Make sure your suit isn't too tight or skirt too short
- Decide what you could wear if you had to 'perform' two days running
- Look for accessories which would enhance your image
- Don't overdo make-up, perfume or aftershave
- De-clutter your handbag so that you can find items easily in it
- Do you have a pen and notebook which is easy to carry and professional? Does your pen work and do you have a standby?

Take with you a copy of your CV, questions you have to ask and any research you've found. Carry directions of how to get there and contact details of the person who organised the interview, in case you run into a problem en route. Charge your mobile phone. Account for potential problems on route when planning your journey times.

Prepare mentally

Preparing for an interview or assessment day takes place at several levels:

- Reviewing what you know about the sector you want to work in and the professional career you've chosen to follow (if relevant); take time to study the websites of professional bodies, relevant newspapers, magazines, and be aware of other useful sources of information.
- Researching the company using every possible resource available to you. Obtain brochures and read them carefully. What impression do they give you of the company? Remind

yourself of the research and development they are involved in, for example.

* Reminding yourself of what you can contribute to that company and how it matches your career goals; review the job description if there is one, to find out how you can contribute to it.
* Practical preparations, such as dressing the part, getting there with time to spare.
* Preparing mentally for questions you may be asked, such as *'What are your strengths?'*, *'Tell us about a team effort you've contributed to and what your role was'*, *'Tell us about yourself!'*.
* Preparing the night before – have an early night, keep alcohol to a minimum and don't eat anything with a strong flavour such as garlic.

Get yourself in the right frame of mind. There's no point in taking baggage that spells the *'Oh poor me, I'll never get a job'* feeling. Why not listen to some music on the way which makes you feel really great? Remember, this interview is a two-way process and a chance for you to ensure that this employer is right for you, just as they need to make sure you're right for them.

Get ready for those questions!

A word about the *'Tell us about yourself'* question. This is not an invitation for you to recite your entire life history. Outline in a couple of sentences where you are now and where you want to be. Keep it short and throw them a couple of points they can pick up on.

What sort of questions should you expect?

* *Why us?*
  Be positive! Select two or three points which made them stand out against their competitors.
* *What did you think of ... e.g. our brochure, website.*
  Be able to back up your views. Can you compare the product or service with those of the competitors in the sector?
* *What do you think you'll be doing in the first year?*
  Comment on the research you've done through talking with other graduates and check your understanding of that role.

Ask questions you have about that first year and your likely career progression.

♦ *What is your perception of yourself?*
This is all about how you think you come over to people. They may ask you how you think you come over to them. How do you want to come over?

♦ *What achievement are you proudest of?*
Think up several achievements; be prepared to talk about the work you put into making them happen.

♦ *What salary are you expecting?*
Outline the research you've done into salaries in the sector, both for new graduates and the industry as a whole. Be prepared to negotiate and remember that the added perks can affect the overall package considerably.

On each point, show you've done your research and back up your answers with well thought out and cohesive answers which are clearly expressed.

You may have a fairly technical interview, if you're looking to work in an area where your degree knowledge and experience will be essential to the core of the job. Go over your research, and be ready to explain technicalities and discuss them. The employer may also look for indications that you understand the ethics surrounding research and reporting.

Questions to ask the interviewers

Try to build up a picture of how your career will fit in with this company and how your role may develop over the next two or three years.

♦ Is this a new position? If not, what is happening to the current post-holder? Are they moving up (a sign of career progression); if it is new, why has it been created?

♦ Ask about the direction the company is taking – and how they see this post contributing to it.

♦ What training and career development will be available to you? Where might you be in three to five years' time? How will this take in any professional qualifications you'd like to work for?

♦ Find out what the next step is in the interview process.

The assessment centre

Many (larger) companies use assessment centres to select their new recruits, lasting a morning or more to see how you'll cope with the demands and stresses of the job. They'll include activities such as team tasks and activities, numeracy and written tests, role-related tests (for example, creating an advert for a product if you were going into advertising), interviews and presentations, and company-specific tests. Look at each exercise from the employer's point of view. What competence or quality are they looking for in the tests they have included? Focus on each one as it appears. Be prepared for the unexpected. You may be asked to present on a subject unknown to you, so that the selectors can see how you handle presenting, debating and working under pressure. Social events may not 'count' towards the assessment, but you'll be quietly watched to see how you interact. Find out what makes your potential work colleagues tick – will you want to be working with them every day under pressure? Drink an absolute minimum of alcohol. You want to be 110 per cent the next day while everyone else is at 80 per cent to 90 per cent.

Personal fit with the team

Well, you either fit, or you don't. And if you don't, it is more to do with the existing team as it is and the person the selectors want to add to it.

To get the fit right, you *may* be called back for several interviews with various team members to get an all-round view of how you'll fit in. Take each opportunity to look closely at your potential colleagues. What would it be like making small talk over the coffee machine? Your colleagues will want to feel comfortable working with you on an assignment through to three in the morning, and you'll want to feel good working alongside them.

Whatever you do, be yourself

It is exhausting to keep up any pretence, and since both you and the company are trying to find out whether the two of you are suited to one another, it is also pointless. If you rapidly come to the conclusion that this company is not for you, then look at that as a positive. Have fun. Welcome the opportunity to test yourself, and be proud that you've got this far.

Offered the post!

Congratulations! Now, take a deep breath. Is this offer really what you want? Will you be happy walking into the organisation every Monday? Can you fulfil your short- and longer-term career goals with it? Is the package right?

If you wish to study for professional qualifications, find out whether the organisation will support you and how quickly you can start on them. In large companies, there may be a training programme for graduates which takes this on board. Be assertive in asking about working for professional qualifications.

Add up perks and benefits

Perks vary, as employers provide increasingly individualised products and services for their employees, and much depends on size and sector, but Table 7.1 shows examples.

Perks and benefits all add up. Find out how your salary is likely to increase in future. Bonuses will vary according to the industry you're in and how well your company – and/or you – perform. Recruitment agencies and salary surveys will tell you a great deal. Look at the kind of positions you would expect to hold in say three

Table 7.1

Private healthcare	Joining bonus
Pension scheme	Personal accident insurance
Holidays	A sum of money to go towards a
Profit and performance-related	course of the employee's choice
bonuses	Sharesave scheme
Buy or sell extra days holiday	Season ticket loan
Flexible working hours	Disability insurance
Child care discounts	Maternity and adoption phase-back
Discounted loans and mortgages	Summer shut down
Relocation packages	Company cars
Car lease schemes/discounts	Subsidised canteen
Financial support for professional	Language training
development	Sport and adventure training
Employee helpline	Insurance
Lifestyle managers	Travel cards
Pet insurance	Payment of professional association
Discretionary bonus	membership fees
Retirement plan	Work-wear
Social activities	

or five years' time and see what the salaries and perks are for them. How different are they to what you would be on now?

Going down the self-employed route

Use professional organisations and networks to get advice, tips and tricks on how to sell your services. Consider yourself as a business – you are – and promote and sell yourself as such. Think back to your work experience days. How did companies you worked with portray themselves? What can you emulate from their approach?

Consider where you're heading financially

Set yourself financial targets. Your bank or a business adviser can help you but you should have a clear idea of your costs, including equipment, your own pay, taxes and insurance, how much items will cost to produce, what you'll charge for your products and services. Consider how you will sell your products and services.

Summary action points

Once you've started sending applications or taking steps towards your proposed first career move after your degree:

1   Keep a record of what you're sending out when; this will help you ascertain whether you're doing enough towards your goal.
2   Assess what is working particularly well and build on that.
3   Get feedback where you can to help you improve your performance the next time.
4   Get involved in a couple of things in life outside of careers and job hunting to help keep a balance in your day and week.

Chapter 8

What's stopping you?
Make it happen!

Frequently in life, things seem to take far too long to go our way. We're waiting for that great job, or know that there isn't going to be one in the region we are in. We're waiting for a lucky break. But all too often, *we* are the people who stop ourselves getting what we want in life.

There are varying scenarios that befall us. For example, you can fall into a rut. You feel that you need a boost with the firepower of a space shuttle to get out of it, followed by a long sustained blast of persistent rocket fuel-type effort. This doesn't just happen in your career, but in relationships with people; perhaps the excitement has gone out of a relationship and you need a super-boost of impetus and excitement to bring it back to life. Perhaps your ability to be spontaneous in life has been overtaken by a preference for the known, safe and comfortable.

It may be that the situation you're in needs one bold, decisive step to get to where you want to be, but you feel like taking that step is like being asked to ski down the steepest, highest most icy slope. You just need to push yourself over the edge and set off, but it's making that first push which freezes you. At this point, we often fear failure and looking a fool in front of others – but we also fear success. We procrastinate from making that call, for fear of being turned down, rejected – but what if we succeed? How will we handle the changes in life that will invariably follow? Will we cope with them?

And then we make glorious plans, and life gets in the way. Family problems, a friend in trouble, illness, death, redundancy, changes thrust upon us, rows, personal discoveries … they all contribute to the fabric of life.

And sometimes, it just seems that we aren't getting anywhere or at least where we want to be as quickly as we wish. Maybe we're waiting for that magic breakthrough – picked at interview, getting funding for that postgraduate course, securing an introduction and follow up meeting with an employer you really want to work for, having a business idea in the shower. We're waiting, confident that these things will happen one day. If we don't stay on top of things and create the right environment and conditions for success, we will probably wait a long time.

It's at times like these that your university days can seem a distant memory, and the weight of debt around your neck heavier than ever.

Don't forget what you went to university for!

If your career plans are taking an age to come to fruition, it can be frustrating to read about people who didn't go to university who say, 'Well, *university wasn't for me, and now I'm a millionaire several times over*'. It can be easy to fall into the trap of blaming others for your current situation, thinking and saying things like 'Well, *the school pushed us into it*', and '*My parents thought it would be a good idea*'.

Five survival tips are:

1   Recognise that there are gifted people who chose not go to university but who have made it up the ladder another route – people reach their potential in their own way and time; what matters is that they get there.
2   Keep everything in perspective – you have as much chance of succeeding as they do.
3   Learn from them.
4   Recall what you got out of your university days. No one can ever take them away from you, or your degree.
5   Focus on where you want to be. Review the progress you've made so far and assess how far you've moved towards achieving your main goals.

Dig deeper into your resources

Whether you fall into a rut or you need to take that one decisive, courageous step, there will always be stages in your life where you need to get tough with yourself and dig deeper within you for the resources you need to achieve the result you want. These resources usually come from within us: energy, focus, clarity of vision and action required, determination, an ability to go out there and get on with it. You've done it before, when you chose to apply to university – and then when you packed and left to head out there. It is *the* time to look afresh into the way you spend your time and energy and to get any unwanted stuff out of the way, such as anything which pulls you down.

Strengthen your resolve

You can choose to change your attitude, approach and luck, and you'll have subconsciously done so many times in life when you felt good about what you were doing, things were going well, you were on course for where you were heading. You may not have been aware that you were doing them. Since then, you probably picked up some bad habits, so it's a good time to make sure they aren't holding you back.

Dump the 'I'll try'. Trying isn't the answer

You can train yourself to think positively and talk positively by watching your language. If you're planning to do something, and think '*I'll try to do this before lunch tomorrow*', then in fact you're unlikely to do it. Think '*I will do this tomorrow before lunch*', and you inject a whole new energy into your focus and you're far more likely to get the thing done. Watch your language for a morning and listen for positive and negative statements. If you're talking more negatively than positively, that will be affecting your mood and manner. You can change that by simply talking more positively and changing your state and the way you're feeling.

What message are you taking on board?

There are times when we don't help ourselves. If we're feeling down, and we watch a depressing television programme in which people are rowing and living mediocre lives, that's going to make us feel worse. If we put a piece of music on we love which makes us feel great and fantastic, then our approach to life changes. Aim for the positive and get a lift from it. Assess the information you receive in any format, dump the negative, work with the positive and strive for the possible and realistic.

Are you caught up in unhelpful patterns of thinking and behaviour?

Examples include criticising yourself, imposing limits or boundaries on the opportunities before you. It involves giving yourself excuses for failing before you start, spending more time on socialising than job hunting, so not giving your career the prominence in your life that it deserves. Perhaps you're being too influenced by listening to generalisations from people who don't know what they're talking about; or you're not applying any creativity to your problem to come up with a solution. Either way, you make the choice whether to take those on board and listen to them, or not.

Misunderstanding of others of what graduates can do for them

This is particularly the case in the SME market, where many bosses cannot keep up to date with all the changes in education at any level, unless they are parents. So make it easy for them. Pay particular attention to your work experience when you write your CV and paint as clear a picture as you can for them of what you can do with clear examples.

Use your problem-solving skills

What can you do to solve the problem?
1 Identify a problem or issue you have now, such as finding a PhD, securing a job offer, or paying off your student debts.
2 Revise where you are now with the problem and identify the solution you want.
3 What is happening right now?
   ♦ What are you doing that is working for you?
   ♦ If you've tried everything, ask yourself:
      ♦ What exactly have you tried?
      ♦ How often have you tried it?
      ♦ When specifically?
      ♦ How much time did you spend over it? How carefully did you do it?
      ♦ What is working well? What isn't?
      ♦ Look back over the last seven days. What did you do on each of those seven days to tackle the problem? If you

only spent an hour on Monday and Wednesday doing something, you can't expect to solve it.

If you learn from this exercise that you're only spending two hours a week making new friends, but that friendship is important to you, then something in your week needs to change. You may need to sacrifice something else to allow room for the change to happen. If you want to work on your portfolio but only devote three hours a week to it, and four evenings to going out with friends, well, your social life is going to look pretty good; your portfolio won't. Devote four evenings to your portfolio, and that fifth evening spent with friends really will feel well deserved.

4   What extra resources and skills do you need to make the change happen? Table 8.1 gives hints!

Where will you get them from?

1   Look for new solutions.
    • Brainstorm every single thing you can think of that you might do to change the situation to make it just the way you want it to be.
    • What one thing do you need to do differently to get the results you need?
    • What else could you do?
    • What other ways could you approach the issue?
    • What would you advise a friend to do?
    • Who do you know who is where you want to be now?
    • What help and advice could they offer you?
    • Who might have experienced the same problem before and could help you unblock where you are now by acting as a mentor to you?
    • If you're running your own company, what could you do to market yourself?

Table 8.1

Extra	Contacts
Skills	Knowledge
Time	Experience
Energy	Influence
Qualifications	Materials
Opportunities	

2   Finally, identify the actions you are prepared to take and when you're going to do them. Pinpoint any support you'll need and identify where you can get that from.

Focus on what you can change

Do something about the things you can change and don't waste time worrying about the things you cannot. When you look at the graduate recruitment market and your life after graduation, identify the things you can influence. If you're self-employed, look at the way you organise your resources because you can influence the way you access and use them.

Pinpoint the missing angle which, once added, could lead to success

What do you need to do to turn your current position into a success and get to where you want to be? For example, you could consider:

1   Working for employers who naturally pick up students with one or two years' experience after university. Why not find out how this route in would help you? Here your alumni associations with your old university could be invaluable.
2   A move into an allied profession for a couple of years and then shift track later, either in your own country or abroad.
3   Relocating now to where the opportunities are – which could be further afield than you like.
4   Working part-time or on short-term stints until you find the right position. Go freelance!
5   Discussing your situation with relevant professional organisations; how flexible are the rules and regulations governing entry to and qualification for membership.
6   Starting your own business. There are lots of opportunities and programmes around for graduates who have business ideas, so find out what support and finance might be on offer and brainstorm that business idea!
7   Joining forces with fellow students from your course and brainstorm the issue together. What could you do collectively to turn the current situation into an opportunity?

Boost your creativity into solving problems and looking for opportunities. Get friends to help you brainstorm, and tap into their knowledge and creativity as well.

Those who put persistent effort into job hunting will succeed in securing the job they want.

The problem with acquiring lower level jobs for the sake of paying off your debts is that they can quickly become long-term roles. You may think you had no alternative: '*There wasn't anything going, so I took this*'. If you're in a geographical area where there seem to be few options, remember that you can also work for companies over the internet.

What practical steps can you take?

There could be *practical* steps you need to take to blow barriers away. Let's look at some of them.

Identify your skills gaps

Look at anything which may boost your employability. Would a particular skill boost your chances of landing the role you crave? Does the agency you've signed up with offer any particular training courses which you could benefit from? If you're temping, talk to your consultant about how you can strengthen your chances to get the job you want. Could you sign up for a professional qualification, for example, while you're looking for the job you want?

In many cases, it won't be your skills which are at a loss. It will be your experience or own organisational skills which are missing. Pinpoint where the gap is between where you are and where you want to be and work out what you need to do to fill it. That gap could consist of particular skills or knowledge.

While waiting for a response ...

One of the traps writers tend to fall into is that they will send out a proposal to a publisher or editor and then wait for a response. What they should be doing is congratulating themselves for getting a proposal out; and then heading straight back to their desks to work on the next one. It's the same with job applications – as soon as you've finished work on one, take a breather and then start on the next.

There will be days when you wonder how on earth you can keep going and when you'll get your lucky break. Stand back and take a long-term approach but ensure that you continually work towards your end goal. Continually add to your experience, your network and your CV. Get your skills and talents out on show; don't tuck them away where no one can see them. Offer to do something for a local charity or business for free – you can talk about it at interview and you could show that you understand the importance of talking to the client and taking their views on board, that you have kept the bottom-line in mind and worked with a team to see an idea through the conception stage and on to completion.

What specialist help is about to help you overcome any barriers you're hitting?

Many groups with special needs now have their own support networks, such as those who have had cancer or heart problems, mature workers, ex-offenders, those returning to the work after a break, people with disabilities, those with learning difficulties, asylum seekers, ethnic minorities, women – the list is simply endless. There are websites set up to help you, such as SKILL at www.skill. org.uk for students and graduates with a disability. Women would do well to plug into the support networks set up for them – examples are under Useful addresses and further information.

How well are you promoting yourself?

Think about the way you're selling yourself in terms of your approach, enthusiasm and passion for the industry. You need to show yourself as a person who can be trusted in the way you handle people and situations. Construct whole sentences, rather than using texting language you'd send to your friends and family. Do not call people 'mate', 'darling' or any other form of endearment. They are not your 'mates'.

Some simple do's and don'ts now follow. Patronising? No – merely included because of employers' comments regarding the lack of basic social skills and manners in many graduates. Practice a warm firm handshake with your friends, looking people in the eye. Keep your shoulders back and square and your head up. You can practice this with strangers you meet in everyday life. When you meet new people, use this handshake and smile. Drop the grunt; you're a graduate: sell yourself as such. Show yourself to be a positive, can do person. Leave the moods at home. We all get black days but there is no need to bring them to work. Do not whine about your current situation or blame past employers, teachers or anyone else for the state you are in. Be positive about going to university. You chose to do it and you gained from it, even though it may not seem like it right now.

Common concerns

I've just got a 2:2 ... You're lucky. I've only got a third ...

Well, many employers are stipulating that, yes, they do want a 2:1 or above and some are quite adamant that they won't consider anyone with lower than that, and if you're looking to do a postgraduate degree, the same will apply – courses will need a first or upper second. But there are plenty of good employers out there who *will* consider lower degrees and your task now is to focus not on what you cannot change but what you can do and influence to get your foot in the door. Focus on what you *can* offer in the way of key skills, personal qualities and drive and motivation. You can promote those and sell them to an employer, and at the end of the day, the employer wants to know what you have to contribute in the future. Could you work for that employer in a couple of years' time after getting some relevant experience behind you?

What about my age?

If you omit your age from your CV or application altogether, employers will wonder even more about your age. Put your date of birth (not your age, e.g. 44 years); it takes longer to work out so people are less likely to bother until later – and put it towards the end of your CV so that the recruiter can be excited about what you've got to offer first. But, there are plenty of good things about being a mature worker and you should show that you mix easily with younger people (not mentioning your own children or grandchildren) in working situations, that you believe you can learn from each other, and get your image checked to make sure you look smart, crisp and fresh. Emphasise your work experience and the good points about maturity; many employers find mature staff more reliable. Show, too, that you can handle change well and that you're not stuck in your ways.

Learn from failure

If you're going to succeed in work, either as an entrepreneur or an employee, you need to be tough and tenacious, and to learn from failure. Two-thirds of all start-ups fail in the first three years, for example, but many successful entrepreneurs point out that failure can be a tremendous learning tool. Failures give up their dreams and goals. They don't learn from the experience because they don't even try to see where they went wrong. They usually fall into the blame culture. Winners and successes may fail, but they learn from their failures and take the experience forward to build future successes.

Analyse failure, and you move forward. View it as part of the learning curve of life, and you'll come out much stronger for it. The tough times in life show you that you have what it takes to survive and come out of situations on top. As you get older, you realise how much you've grown from all those difficult times in work and personal life. We all hit rough patches in life, like an aircraft going through turbulence, but we usually come out of it all the stronger for it. When you look back on something in this context, if you learn from an experience, you can hardly describe it as failure.

Don't take failure personally

If you didn't get that much cherished job you wanted, perhaps it simply wasn't meant to be – maybe someone else was simply a better fit for the post and the company. Take your 'failure' with you in the next interview and you won't win any friends. Invest in a punch bag or get aggressive in the gym instead, get feedback if you can and review your performance yourself.

Ten survival steps to coping with failure:

1   Have faith in yourself – there will be that perfect position for you somewhere out there, but you need to know what you're looking for. Keep focused and keep trying.
2   Keep knocking at doors. Get help and support around you, both experts in the field and your friends and family.

3   Ask for advice on turning those potential applications into sure bets.

4   Look for new strategies.

5   Keep a sense of perspective.

6   Don't turn to comfort eating, drink or drugs. It won't change anything. Keep healthy.

7   Learn from those who have failed but picked themselves up and gone on to be successful.

8   Obstacles in our way are often our unwillingness to say 'no' to people, or our belief in ourselves as much as anything real or physical.

9   Push yourself out of your boundary zone at every opportunity you get. You'll be surprised how much you can achieve.

10   Live life differently if you can. A fresh approach works wonders and avoids your getting stuck in a rut.

Self-employed and ...

Someone's pinched my idea!

If you're going to create and implement designs or ideas or anything of that ilk, you'll want copyrights, patents and trademarks. Protect your own ideas and designs by making full use of the support available to you, such as:

Institute of Trade Mark Attorneys
www.itma.org.uk

Usability Professionals' Association
www.upassoc.org

Own It
www.own-it.org

The Writers' Copyright Association
www.wcauk.com/
(This body protects the rights of writers.)

Webmasters Copyright Association
www.wmcaglobal.org/

Finally, the Charter on Intellectual Property promoted a new user-friendly way of handing out intellectual property rights in

2005, written by an international group of artists, scientists, lawyers, politicians, academics and business experts.

Access to finance

Apart from the obvious organisations to try, such as professional bodies and trade organisations, don't forget to tap into the various initiatives which may be taking part in your country or region to encourage growth and regeneration.

Needing help on a particular aspect of your journey?

Certainly in the UK, cluster groups exist to enable people in a field to meet with colleagues and other like-minded professionals, share best practice and benefit from each other's experience, expertise and network. Many of these will have individuals you can tap into for expert help and advice. These vary in the way in which they are organised and in the help they can give you. BusinessLink's network can help you, first, set up your own business, and second, to grow the business, with help and information in areas such as exploiting your ideas, employing people, health, safety and premises, international trade, finance, grants and guidance on the rules and regulations applying to businesses in the creative industries sector.

Not getting the business?

If you're running your own business but you're not getting the sales you want, think about what is working for you and what is not. Contact people who have decided not to buy or pursue your product or service, and ask for some feedback. Is there anything in your sales pitch which did not endear them to your sale? What could you have done differently to achieve a different outcome? If there was nothing, were you looking in the right place for clients to start with, or pricing it properly? Get business advice, either from local business advisers or specific industry bodies.

Persist and persevere, but learn and listen to where you're going wrong and then put it right next time.

Summary action points

Identify barriers and obstacles and then do something about them through creative thinking.

1 Identify what barriers and obstacles you have ahead of you which may hinder you achieving your goals.
2 Now pinpoint as many ways to tackle them as you can.
3 Identify the one which will work best for you and do it.

Chapter 9

Moving on ... Your future

No matter who you work for, careers and businesses need nurturing and loving care just like any relationship in life. Devote time and energy to them, and they will blossom. Give your career loving care, or it will degenerate into just a job.

First, you need to walk before you can run

So you're about to start work, and you know you're expected to hit the ground running. How can you make this transition easier for yourself?

Plan your wardrobe in advance for each working day in your first week and check that it is clean and pressed. Get meals in to save yourself the hassle of shopping for meals on the way home after work. Spend some time exploring the area where your company is located, so that you know where the nearest chemist, supermarket, and so on, are.

Starting work in any company can be frustrating for a few weeks. If you can make a visit for a couple of hours before you officially start, that will help and give you a chance to check the dress code once more and learn the basic layout of the office, meet people and acquire some sort of familiarity with the place you're going to be working in. You want to prove yourself and settle in. Yet being in a new work environment is just like being in a country you've never visited before, with lots to learn: how the computer system works, and whether there is an intranet; whose approval you need for what; who the key decision-makers are; and what people do at lunch time. You'll also learn who is who, what is where, and try to remember names and what people do. Why not ask for a buddy who can help and guide you, someone you can turn to for advice and information?

Make an impact!

Eight ways to do this are:

1 Be friendly without gushing. Don't call people 'mate'. They are not your mates (yet); they are work colleagues. Remember that most people remember their first day; they want to put you at ease. As you meet people, offer a friendly firm handshake and a smile.

2 Listen and learn how things work before you dive in with comments; find out the history behind something which looks strange to you before you make suggestions.

3 Ask people questions about themselves and their role. '*What do you do? How long have you been here?*'. It's a great way to learn who does what.

4 Be willing to stay late to get things done.

5 Double-check your work for accuracy.

6 Prove you're a safe pair of hands to be trusted and a team player who fits in.

7 Be ready to begin at the bottom and use the opportunity to learn as much as you can about the way it functions there.

8 Get social. Hang about and talk to people over the coffee machine, have lunch or drink with them. They are human, after all, and you're hoping for a relatively long association with them as friends and colleagues.

Check company policy regarding mobiles and personal emails; and before you put any information online, such as blogs, consider how it could be used. Keep your own counsel; don't shoot your mouth off. Pick your confidantes and true work friends with care. Confidential means just that.

As well as working, there's the added stress of handling full-time work five days a week, and doing all those small but essential tasks needed to keep life ticking along smoothly. If you spend eight hours a day sleeping (56 hours a week) and nine hours a day working, including the commute to work, that leaves you with 67 hours a week to do your admin, pay bills and do the banking; do the laundry and ironing, clean and shop, cook, eat and wash up, take care of personal hygiene and, more occasionally, have check ups with doctor, dentist, hygienist, gynaecologist, and take the car to the garage for an MOT. You'll also want time to enjoy activities such as socialising, catching up with old mates, remembering your parents, leisure hobbies, exercise, weekends away and that all important 'me' down time to relax and recharge your batteries. On top of all that, you may have enrolled for further learning or work towards a professional qualification.

So what happens next?

There are a number of 'what' and 'where' and 'how' questions here. What have you achieved so far, and where do you see your career going next? Are there any potential barriers or obstacles which might hinder your progress? Can you acquire extra skills to give you more openings in the employment market?

A dogged, persistent effort is essential to take you to career success, in which these skills will be essential:

- Self-awareness
  Know your strengths, weaknesses, passions, ambitions, values and needs
- Self-promotion
  Raising your profile in the organisation and sector
- Exploring and creating opportunities
  Being proactive in taking responsibility for your own career development
- Decision-making and action planning
  Informed, decisive decisions that will take you in the right direction and working out what needs to be done when
- Coping with uncertainty
  Redundancy, restructuring, new clients, new tomorrows
- Transfer of skills
  Thinking laterally and broadly, applying the commonalities to the workplace and life
- Self-belief and confidence
  Yes, you can do it!
- Willingness to learn
  New products, new technology, new skills

- Commitment/dependability
  Everyone knows you're a safe pair of hands and management and your own staff trust you
- Self-motivation
  You have drive, enthusiasm, and take the initiative
- Co-operation
  People want to have you on board their team
- In the know about new developments in the field
  It shows you're well up to date.

Plot and plan your next steps, pinpointing the learning and experiences you will need to get to the next stage, especially if you are in a lower level position than you had hoped for after leaving university. Keep your career aspirations at the forefront of your mind. While everyone else sleeps and parties, work towards them. You'll soon climb the career ladder through your own dogged determination and persistence and perseverance. Failures in life give up. Winners persist.

Getting promoted

If you want to move up, plan for it and lay the ground! For instance, if you get the chance to train up any new staff or take responsibility for a group, do it; you can show off your management potential. Ensure your team knows what is expected of them and treat them all fairly and equally. When you delegate, check that people know what needs to be done, by when, and ask if they need any help. Listen to their feedback and questions. Show how effective you are and tell your boss about the results you're getting.

That routine lab position you took will give you the chance to acquire invaluable experience and skills for your next role, such as working to quality standards and working to tight deadlines. Some of these are not always possible to pick up in an academic setting, although governments worldwide are striving to encourage business and academia in their widest sense to work and collaborate together, sharing ideas, innovations, research, skills, knowledge and expertise. You may be happy to remain in a lab environment, perhaps managing a number of staff, or move to areas such as quality assessment and control.

Smooth the path to promotion

Ensure you have a regular review to assess your performance and how you're progressing. Out of the office, ask yourself if you're on track to achieve your career goals in the timescale you want with your employer. Review the way you work; how can you handle your workload more effectively and time efficiently while maintaining or improving your performance? Ensure you understand what any new role is about and what it contributes to the organisation's vision, and ensure that your team is properly trained and motivated to achieve the results expected of them. As you progress up the ladder, wear a managerial hat rather than a technical one, and take a higher helicopter view looking at the bigger picture. Delegate where you can, developing those you supervise through coaching, mentoring and one-to-one training. Assess whether you need any extra skills or qualifications to progress your path, such as an MBA, postgraduate or professional studies. And consider how changes at work could provide you with new opportunities.

A strong network right across a company could smooth your path into new roles and it will raise your profile. Get on a committee so that other people can see how you perform. Keep up to date with everything that is going on in your sector and in your clients' sector. Be the first to know. Finally, dress for the role you aspire to, not the role you're in.

Look to see what is going on in your sector

Attend events, conferences, lectures, lunches, anything you can which will help you build your network and keep in touch with what is happening in your sector. Again, professional bodies will have details of what is happening in your region, although of course you could always travel further afield to something which really grabs your interest. Websites such as www.sciencedirect.com can alert you to new journal issues, while www.trends.com has 15 titles covering biomedical and life science news.

It's worth mentioning that as mergers between companies and the take-over of small companies by their larger counterparts is on the increase, watch out for what is happening in your sector and be prepared to handle the situation accordingly. A merger or take-over could spell survival, redundancy, promotion or a sideways move for you and the way you handle the circumstances and approach the outcome can mean all the difference between a halted career and a move onwards to a good next step.

Networking is as important outside a company as you move up the career ladder as it is in it. Many senior managers and professionals are recruited through recruitment agencies, head-hunters and search companies. These companies receive assignments from organisations which have roles to fill. Head-hunters will call around their contacts in the industry to see if they know of anyone who might fit the bill. Someone in your network may think of you …

Know your worth

Prior to your reviews, find out what the industry pays someone with your experience and qualifications, but keep in mind that that perks can make a big difference to the value of your overall package. Many agencies have salary reviews on their websites. The *New Scientist Careers Guide*, available as a download from the New Scientist website, includes a salary review and perks comparison between industry and academia and different levels of employee. Pull all your evidence together of what you've contributed to the company, plus your research on pay and put your case forward for a rise if you want one. Don't expect to get an immediate answer and don't be surprised if the answer is 'no', but be prepared to negotiate. Perhaps the company will pay for you to undertake further studies instead of having more pay. There are ways and means to enhance your overall package.

Make the most of your professional body

Many professional bodies have different types of membership depending on the stage you are at in your career. Are you raising your level of membership to match your experience? Can you get involved in a working group to boost your network and knowledge and influence the direction it takes, or get involved in your region and give something back to those young professionals coming through?

Getting connected

These websites may help you:

+ www.scienceresearch.com – a one stop resource for scientific research, with links to publishing groups, magazines, journals and books;

* www.123biotech.com – covers biotechnology, pharmaceutical industry, science articles, life science, and clinical research. There are links to websites for postgraduates, life science jobs, other useful websites and news;
* www.sciencemediacentre.org – talk to the media when your area of speciality hits the headlines!

Continue to train and learn

Employers expect to find that you've been taught to use that fine brain of yours and they will want to see lots of initiative. Challenge your brain and creative thinking processes at every opportunity you get: use it or lose it! At university, you pushed your brain out of its comfort zone, both academically and in living the experience. This was why, for most people, university is a great experience. The unhappy people at work are bored; they've stopped pushing themselves, learning, growing and developing and expect someone else to take the responsibility to make their career dreams happen. Which category do you want to fall into?

As a graduate, you're more likely to ask for training because you are used to identifying your own training and learning needs and making sure they are met. Your university studies will have taught you how to learn through many methods, which will prepare you well for training at work. You can learn informally, by reading books and articles, taking correspondence courses, accessing learning materials on the internet and also more formally for a qualification. You can also learn by being shown how to do things and then practising them, or through one-to-one training and coaching sessions with a manager or boss. Identify where your skills gaps are and what you need to do to close that gap. Think about skills which will give your company or your own performance an added dimension and get you ahead of the rest.

Governments worldwide are seeking to boost their citizens' skills and capabilities in the battle to be competitive. In the UK for example, Sector Skills Councils (www.ssda.org.uk) are working to ensure that employers have the skills they need in the workforce for the future. Examples are:

* SEMTA (science, engineering and manufacturing and technology industries at www.semta.org.uk);

* Lantra (the environmental and land based industries at www. lantra.co.uk);
* Energy and Utility Skills (www.euskills.co.uk);
* Skills for Health (www.skillsforhealth.org.uk).

Continued Professional Development (CPD)

Visit professional bodies to find out what is on offer to:

1   Update your job-related skills and technical knowledge;
2   Boost your transferable skills and ability to handle people
3   Develop your business – many organisations have helpful workshops and training for the self-employed;
4   Prove you're up to date.

It may be a requirement that you continue with learning and training after you've achieved professional status on an annual basis to keep you up to date with new technologies, skills and developments and knowledge. Discuss your needs with your employer or contact the most relevant professional body to identify what you need to do to meet this commitment. Plan your CPD well ahead in the year to ensure that you meet any necessary targets and can truly select something which will enhance your learning. Make good use of professional bodies, their experience and knowledge. Many provide mentors to help students through.

Studying for professional qualifications or a part-time postgraduate degree?

Identify the training and learning you need to get to where you want to be or to do your role more effectively and to meet your career aspirations. If you decide to study for professional qualifications, talk to your current employer, who may be willing to support you with study leave or financial support, perhaps paying for all or part of the course, or your study materials or examinations. Show how your studies will boost your effectiveness on the job and benefit your employer, so that you present a 'win–win' situation.

Studying whilst in full-time work requires real motivation and dedication and there will be many times when you feel like doing something other than hitting the books. Identify the time of day which you work best at, and acknowledge that there will be many occasions when you just feel like switching off and doing something totally different or even nothing at all. It can be helpful to just promise yourself half an hour or even 20 minutes' work, only to find that once you get going, you're happy to do an hour. Get advice from those who've done it on how they handled work and full-time study. Find a quiet place and time to study and reward yourself afterwards. Continually remind yourself of the reason you're studying for the qualifications at the forefront of your mind, because it will keep you going when times get tough.

If you choose to have a career related to biology, you could look at acquiring the European professional title, *EurProBiol*. The European Countries Biological Association has details (see Useful Addresses and Further Information).

What about an MBA?

If you're considering doing an MBA, contact the Association of MBAs (see Useful Addresses and Further Information) which represents the international MBA community: its students, graduates, schools, businesses and employers. The Association promotes the MBA as a leading management qualification and aims to encourage management education at postgraduate level to create highly competent professional managers. MBAs benefit those students who want to be effective at a strategic level, and provide an invaluable opportunity to develop your career. You'll develop a portfolio of managerial tools and techniques as well as the 'softer' skills needed to succeed as a manager such as an entrepreneurial spirit, dedication, commitment and professionalism. In some sectors, the MBA is a must have and it will help your chances of success, whether you decide to go on and work for someone else or to set up on your own.

It's not working out!

If you think things aren't going well as you try to settle into a new job, give it time. Ask for feedback on your performance. Can you pinpoint what it is that is not quite right? Do you need more support from your boss or line-manager? At the least, view this role as a stepping stone to something better. It can take a couple of attempts to get the match of employer and role right; many employers appreciate that. In fact, some even deliberately pick up graduates a couple of years after their degree, with the understanding that their first post may not have lived up to their expectations or worked out. But think before you move. You don't want to acquire a reputation as a job-hopper.

Leaving your current employer

Before you even think about handing in your notice, ensure that there are absolutely no other opportunities at your current company. Consider what have you done to create opportunities for expanding your role and taking on new projects and responsibilities? What is right with the job you have now? Often there's plenty we like about our work, and it's the bits we don't like that we tend to focus on and gripe about.

Now look forward. Have your ambitions got lost in the current role you're in? Before you decide whether you can achieve them with your current employer, talk to your boss and/or HR and put an action plan together to help you get back on track. If your current employer cannot meet your future aspirations, *then* research a move to another organisation or setting up on your own. Get the new deal signed before giving in your notice. Be discreet; don't work at your CV in work time on a work PC. Use the internet and specialist agencies, your network and company websites to help you find that next right move. Generally a two or three year period with an employer shows that you're looking to progress your career without being a job-hopper.

Changing your career

Ensure that you are really ready for a change and not simply fed up with the job you're in at the moment or in need of new responsibilities. Changing career can offer an amazing journey, which demands self-discovery and the freedom to think about what you really want to do. Identify the things you're drawn towards and feel passionate about, and network to get to the people who can give you great advice on how to make your move happen. Be honest and open with potential employers about your reasons for a career change – they will want to know that you've thought this move through and that your new path isn't just a six-month wonder. Use your covering letter to explain your move.

Of course, your new career could be achieved through a sideways move with the company you are currently working for, but into a new role.

Relocating abroad

When you're looking at any financial provision for your future, check to see what the taxation implications are if you move about. How will working abroad affect any pension due to you later in life, for example, be it state or private? A good accountant with international experience should be able to help you. Shop around to get the best deal you can.

If you choose to work abroad, remember that you may want to return home later. Keep an eye on developments there to ensure that time spent away or changes in professional organisations' ground rules for membership and qualification don't prevent you from entering your chosen career back home, say 20 years later.

If you're looking to move within the EU, then check out the European Countries Biologists Organisation, which seeks to facilitate the free movement of biologists within Europe, and to promote cooperation between national biological associations in Europe. You could also visit www.expatnetwork.com/ which is invaluable for expatriates working around the world, with a salary survey, international jobs, lifestyle, money, health and more. There's even an Expats for Kids club!

Just biding your time?

If you're not on a professional career with a specific path, it's even more important to stop and take stock from time to time. Without such a step, you'll be like a ship's captain without a chart.

Seven point plan to taking action:

1   Stop.
2   Consider where you are in relation to where you're heading.
3   Does your original goal need amending or changing in any way?
4   What do you need to do more of to boost your progress?
5   Who do you need to help you?
6   What steps do you need to take?
7   When will you take them?

So you've set up your own business and want to go for growth?

As you grow, delegate as much as you can, so that you're free to focus on the business. One possibility is to hire a virtual assistant, whom you would pay by the hour. Visit www.iava.org.uk to find out more. Consider:

- What have you achieved to date?
- What are your strengths, weaknesses, opportunities and threats?
- Where do you see your business going in the next year? The next five years?
- What extra resources do you need, e.g. time, money, equipment?
- Who can help you with that?
- What new products or services are you creating/innovating?
- What extra staff if any do you need and how will you find and employ them?
- What are you doing to build your niche and brand?
- What are your financial targets for the year?
- How much time are you devoting to business planning?
- What can you outsource, leaving yourself to focus on developing the business?
- What are you doing to get feedback from your customers to enhance the prospect of repeat business?
- Which marketing methods are proving to be most effective?
- What three new ways can you think of to market your business?
- What three new things can you think of to surprise and delight existing customers?
- Which comes first: business or lifestyle?

From the perks listed on page 109, pinpoint which really matter to you long term and immediately, and then work them into your business plan to ensure they happen.

Looking to leave the day job behind

You may be working in the day to get some money coming in and tackling your 'real' job at night, hoping to resign when you hit a breakthrough. If this sounds like you, make sure your 'night' job is honestly going places by asking the following questions:

* What have you achieved overall so far?
* What is working well?
* Where can you create more time in your day?
* Where do you want to be in six months' time?
* What will you need to do to make that happen?
* Who can help you further?
* What do you need to do to move your business to the next stage?
* How can you add value to your products and services so as to bring in extra income and enable you to focus more on the business and reduce the time you're spending on the day job?

Finally, keep your bank informed of how things are going. It's better to talk to them when problems are small rather than until they are haunting your dreams at night.

That's life!

Handling misconceptions of the role

It may be a huge source of annoyance to you that people find it hard to understand what goes on in your world, just as they may find it equally frustrating that you do not comprehend theirs. The world of science can be specially misunderstood; many people have a vague vision of a Bunsen burner in a lab from memories of their school days, when they didn't do well at science and now a fear of looking stupid when you start talking about your day prevents them from asking the questions they could ask. Use easy examples of the impact your work has and describe how you are involved in the process.

Giving something back

Do you want to give something back, and if so, how? For example, would you like to:

1   Help shape the future careers of young professionals coming through by offering advice, being a mentor and coach to them?

2   Be a role model or a case study on a website or in a prospectus. What words of wisdom and encouragement would you offer to young people coming through the education system, for example? There are a number of women's science websites, for example, listed in Useful Addresses and Further Information, which have role models. Could you be one of them?

3   Get involved in the international community, by contributing to a network?

4   Raise the profile of science (or, indeed, any other career you choose to go into) by giving talks at schools, helping out at careers events or offering work experience placements to young people?

5   Use your skills voluntarily, for example, to do conservation work, with an organisation such as www.earthwatch.org?

Working with universities

What could you do to give something back to your old university? You could:

1   Help graduates coming through the system, perhaps by contributing towards the delivery of careers support to those in your subject areas. Why not invite a member from the careers team into your company for a day so that they can see exactly what goes on?

2   Ask university staff to deliver continued professional development sessions at any local events you're holding.

3   Benefit from the research and development being undertaken by the universities themselves – they have more time to do it.

4   Join forces with the relevant department at your university by working on a project, an innovation or some research together.

5   Help graduates coming through the system by offering them a project which is relavant to their studies that your company needs doing but does not have the internal resources to do.

6   Give students a real life work project to get stuck into.

Flexibility and adaptability go a long way to making the most of life

You may be merrily making your way through your career and then something happens which changes everything for you at a stroke.

Ten events which could change your life and your career:

1   You meet your future partner; and life is never the same.
2   Your create a baby and parenthood is on the way.
3   You hit on a business or social idea which, if implemented, will really make a difference.
4   You or one or your relatives or a friend falls seriously ill or has an accident and needs special care and love; plus it makes you rethink.
5   You get head-hunted.
6   A major world event makes you rethink life.
7   You volunteer for a cause you believe in.
8   You decide to live abroad.
9   You win the lottery.
10   You take the decision that you want to live a higher quality life and set about doing just that.

Summary action points

Take responsibility for enhancing your own employability:

1   Keep a track of any ways in which recruitments methods for your sector change.
2   Who are the key players in the market you're in for recruitment? Who are the main agencies?
3   Don't stay with an employer if they're not enabling you to meet your career goals but have a discussion with them first before handing in your notice.

Chapter 10

Here's to life!

Take a holistic view of your life, and good health and happiness are more likely to be yours. Take a narrow, focused view of it, concentrating on only one aspect, and the others areas will suffer. If you're not fit and healthy, it will be harder to maintain a peak performance at work, which could make all the difference to whether you get that promotion or not. Continually review your life and consider questions such as:

- What do you want in your life besides your career?
- Who do you want in your life?
- What are you doing to enjoy life?
- What are you doing to pay off your loans?
- What are you doing to start building financial security for yourself?

Life is not a dress rehearsal. Make time for those things which matter to you most, such as family, friends and fun. The way you manage your resources – time, energy, money, health and relationships – can make a huge difference to the quality of life you enjoy. What are the things you want in your life to be happy and fulfilled? Do any of the examples in Table 10.1 feature?

From the day we are born, life often gets in the way, throwing trials, tribulations and challenges at us. Working towards some 'wants' and 'must haves' in your life may demand that you 'park' other things aside for several weeks or months while you focus on them or a project that is of particular importance to you – such as your wedding day or training for a marathon. A balance helps to keep things in perspective; indeed, work–life balance is one hot topic as individuals struggle to find ways to cope with the demands

Table 10.1

Family – perhaps children	Key relationships and roles
Pets	Fun and laughter
Friends	Volunteering
Travel	Cultural and leisure activities
Dreams come true	Nature
Adventure	Excitement
Material goods	A good sex life
Achievements	Nice place to live
Financial assets	Solid retirement plans
Health and vitality	Great memories
Spirituality	Other

of work and personal commitments to family and friends. Table 10.2 gives suggestions as to where balance is important.

How balanced is your life?

Every year, do a stock-take and ask yourself whether your work–life balance is as you want it to be. How content you are with each area of your life which is important to you? Are there any areas or aspects of your life that you want to change?

Try this exercise to assess how well balanced your life is. For each of the categories you ticked in Table 10.1, consider:

1   How satisfied are you right now with each one? Rate them individually from 0 to 10. Totally satisfied earns a 10; complete dissatisfaction at the centre a 0.
2   How does your life look? How many segments are a 10?
3   Which ones need working on (i.e. are below a 7)? What would they have to be like for you to rank them as a 10?
4   What do you need to do to make that happen?
5   What will you do to make them happen and when?

Table 10.2

Work	and	Leisure
Work	and	Holidays
Rest	and	Exercise
Healthy food	and	A bit of what you fancy
Smooth running of life	and	Challenges
Certainty	and	Uncertainty

You can repeat this exercise annually, enabling you to make the changes you want in your life through a continual process of making sure that every one is a 10, or at least working to it. You can also do it with each element you deem important, so that you may choose to divide health and fitness into areas such as fitness, healthy eating, chill time, stretching and flexibility and smoking, each with a grade out of 10 for current satisfaction. Then you know what you need to work on.

But work's taken over my life!

More employees are now finding that short breaks recharge their batteries quite adequately without a huge panic about sorting out the in-tray before they go and when they get back. Too many don't take their full holiday allowance, *'I'm too busy at work'*. Very few of us can keep going at premium performance without having some sort of regular break built into the day. Our own bodies have their own needs; one person may be able to do with very little sleep, while others need a lot. If you don't listen to your body, sooner or later it will pay you back when you least need it to remind you that it has needs too, such as *proper* rest and recuperation. You're not indispensable. Sad to say this, but if you were killed by a bus today, your company or organisation *would* go on without you. If you don't look after yourself, you are unlikely to be able to take care of others.

Long hours are the norm in some sectors, but it can be easy to fall into the trap of doing long hours for the sake of it. The person who never takes a lunch break can rarely work at the same performance level throughout the day. The person who always takes a break away from the phone, email and work environment can only find her performance enhanced. No excuses! Walk around the block for 20 minutes and boost your heart beat, reduce your stress levels, keep that weight down *and* boost your mood.

Stress

The right sort of stress can help you live longer. Mild to moderate stress increases the production of brain cells, enabling them to function at peak capacity, so if you want to live life to a peak performance, get stressed but in the right way – it makes your body and mind stronger.

Beneficial stress gives you recovery time and a sense of accomplishment afterwards. It challenges you, although you may complain about it at the time. The bad stuff is prolonged, repeated, sustained and unrewarding. You need to find the gap somewhere between the two and build it into your daily life. Look for activities which reward and stimulate you, such as a run before work, studying in the evenings or voluntary work at weekends.

Get out of your comfort zone and take part in something which isn't routine and predictable or effortless. The more you look for these sorts of activities, the more you'll benefit. Collapsing in front of the TV after a day's work with a glass of wine isn't necessarily beneficial. Playing some sort of sport or going to adult education is. It's important to face stress or challenges mentally, physically, socially and spiritually. Give yourself proper 'chill' time. Don't waste time dwelling on the problems, demands and negatives of life – think about the pleasure, variety and vigour that challenges bring us and you'll feel much more alert and in control. Many challenges arrive through the roles we choose to play in life.

What roles do you want to play?

We all have roles in life and they all tend to appear at different times. Table 10.3 shows roles most of us experience in our lives.

Table 10.3

Parent	Friend
Son/daughter	Volunteer
Manager	Leader
Supervisor	Confidante
Doer	Thinker
Teacher	Adviser
Loner	Niece/nephew
Aunt/uncle	Grandparent
Actor	Diplomat
Neighbour	Carer
Sister/brother	Cousin
Good Samaritan	Hero

Our roles and relationships and the responsibilities that come with them intertwine with careers more than any other aspect of life. Which comes first: career or ageing relative? The presentation or a sick child? The school play or your squash game? The carer in us may play a key role and take centre stage in our lives while our parents get older and need decisions to be made for them. The parent has a lifelong role, but spends more time on it in the early years of a child's life and that role changes as life progresses, such that their children become their friends in adulthood. Our relationship with our siblings changes, too, particularly as we all settle down into adult life and face the challenges dealing with ageing parents brings.

Our friends also change. We keep some throughout life; others we see enter at different stages and then leave, as if they came for a reason. Perhaps they were there to teach us something, to make us laugh at a time when we felt low, to make us feel good about ourselves, or just ... because. We need friends, both as an individual in our own right and later when we may have a partner. Friends help you keep things in perspective. A true friend is there for the good and bad times and will see you through.

If we're to have successful, empowering relationships, we need to put boundaries on what we will and won't do in our role. We may tire of the friend who calls us just once too often in the early hours of the morning, distraught over a break-up. We may be fed up of being the only sibling who makes an effort with our parents, while our siblings bleat that they are 'too busy'. Assertiveness is important if friendships and relationships are to thrive and grow. Saying 'yes' to keep the peace usually leads to feelings of resentment and disappointment in ourselves for not having the courage to say what we really want to say. Saying 'no' is a sign that we feel confident enough in ourselves to say what we mean and, crucially, that we care about ourselves and what we undertake in life.

The ability to manage yourself and others impacts on your ability to be personally effective in work and life. For example, if you have children, you will need to motivate them and get the family working as a team on projects to create a cohesive family unit. There will be times when you need to manage your own temper, when they do something which drives you to distraction for the hundredth time. Similarly, you will need to manage your client relationships at the office. If someone asks you for a piece of work which you know you cannot do within the timescale they give you, you will need to manage that and talk to them about it. You've learnt to manage people, situations and life at university and in your past life experience.

Develop your ability to handle people:

1   Identify your boundaries in any relationship – the rules you feel comfortable with – and stick to them.
2   Look at things from the other person's point of view. Put yourself in their shoes to get an idea for how they are feeling.
3   Remember that you cannot change other people – but you certainly *can* change the way you behave towards them.
4   Work on what you know you *can* influence, as opposed to the things you cannot.

Use your resources effectively

We have a tremendous amount of resources at our disposal, from mind-mapping to help creativity, speed reading to enable us to acquire knowledge more quickly, our memory to help retain it, meditation to help us focus and exercise to boost our energy. But the thing most people want more of today is time.

Is your time management letting you down?

'*I haven't got time*' is a common complaint. So run a quality control check on the way you spend your time.

- Track the ways in which you spend your time.
- Look back at your wheel of life and the activities you identified as important to you.
- How much of the 168 hours a week do you spend on them?
- Decide what to do about any imbalance.
- Track the way you spend your time for a week. In particular, track wasted time caused by any of the examples given in Table 10.4.

Identify the three which waste most time for you and how much time they take up. What difference would it make if you didn't spend time on them? What are you going to do to get rid of them and what will you do with your time instead?

Undertake exercises like this while you're still at university, when you've graduated and later on when you have work, family

Table 10.4

Negative people/thoughts	Missing deadlines
Unanswered messages	Difficulty communicating
Outstanding letters and bills	Computer illiterate
Lacking confidence	Non-assertiveness
Unnecessary texting/emailing	Information overload
Losing things, e.g. keys	Smoking
Surfing the internet	Drink and drugs
Broken items	Gambling
Too much TV	Fears
Poor sleep	Anxieties
Flitting from one thing to another	Doubts
without any real focus	Unnecessary meetings

and house maintenance responsibilities, commuting, studying for professional qualifications, and have social and leisure activities to fit in. You can also apply it to your working day to find out how you can use your time more effectively at work.

Do the same exercise with money:

- What financial base do you want to build up in the future?
- What do you need to do to make that happen?
- What is getting in the way?

Identify the financial resources you want and then you can start making them happen. Some items are essentials, such as a property to rent or buy, living costs and tax and state demands, e.g. national insurance. After that, savings are usually a wise move for that rainy day, and so is insurance. There are also a whole range of investments, savings accounts, stocks and shares which are best discussed with a financial adviser.

Ten ways to review your finances continually:

1. Where is your money going?
2. Which items are essential, important, nice to have?
3. Where can you cut back?
4. What will you do to make that happen?
5. Which items do you no longer need and could sell?
6. How could you make more money? Examples include focusing on career development so that your salary increases.
7. Who can help you sort out your debts and finances?
8. What do banks and building societies offer graduates?

9   What realistically can you achieve in the next week, six months and three to five years? How can you capitalise on that? Put any unexpected windfalls such as a bonus or present into paying off your loan straight away.

10   How rigorously are you making your money work for you?

Make your money work for you. Be proactive in looking for the best deal, the highest interest rates which suit your needs, the lowest loan rates, and keep looking. Do a three monthly financial MOT and reward yourself for your financial acumen. The more you go up the career ladder, the greater the perks and salary. Working for professional qualifications at night will not only boost your employability, it will keep you away from expensive bars and nightclubs, keep your money in your pocket and enable you to pay off your loans and debts faster.

Most people continually believe they are short of time and money, but don't proactively do enough specifically about it. It takes discipline, effort and creative thinking to sort out your finances. Paying off a loan doesn't take forever, even though it may seem like it. Much depends on *how* focused you are in paying off your loans. And if you nurture your career, your financial status should get better as you're rewarded for your efforts. Careers take up around 48 weeks a year out of 52 and subsequently impact on your overall quality of life, so surely they are worth the effort and dedication?

Living at home with your parents after university?

Many young people are moving back home after university to save money, to pay off debts and for an assortment of other reasons. But what other options do you have apart from moving back in with your parent(s)? Could you get in touch with other graduates in the area or on the same graduate trainee scheme in your company who are in the same boat and flat-share, or live abroad in a country where graduates are welcomed and it is easier to get on the housing ladder? If you still decide to return home (perhaps you never left), work out a financial arrangement so that you pay your parent(s) rent (even if it is a very small amount) – you need to keep in the habit of budgeting for your housing. And arrange with them what your contribution will be towards the house-keeping, be it cleaning, washing, helping in the garden, cooking a meal a couple of times a week. Don't fall back into the ways of a teenager having everything done for you. You've moved on from that and so have your parents, so don't use your parents' home: sit up, take some responsibility and *contribute* to it. Sit down and agree a few house rules (just as you would have had at university with your flat mates) to keep everyone happy and remember to practice the art of negotiation and compromise. Finally, consider:

+ How long ... do you intend to stay with your parents? Give yourself a deadline to leave and stick to it. Do you want to be living with them when you're 40?
+ How much ... of your student debt will you have paid off by that time? How will you do it?
+ What ... will you have achieved in your career by then and how will that have boosted your income to help you start building a financial base?

Finally, when the time does come to move out, why not get your parents a small gift as a token of appreciation for their help over the years? Parents are usually very happy to help out their offspring – but it is always nice to be appreciated and thanked.

Don't forget the wild and wacky

What would your life be like if you drew up a list of all the things you wanted to do and achieved them before your eightieth birthday? What a glorious blaze of memories you could have to look back on as your older years set in!

List the things you want to do and the reasons *not* to do them will fade into the background. You'll be filled with a tremendous energy and enthusiasm, passion and excitement as you start identifying how and when you're going to do it all. Writing your list down enhances your determination to make your items happen. Keep your list where you can easily see it *frequently*. Show your list to those who are important to you in your life. Suggest they draw up a list of their own, and compare notes. Are there things you can do together? Can you give each other the time and space required to make them happen? You need to make sure that those you love don't constrain you in a plant pot, so that your roots cannot spread out and grow. If they do limit you, it may be time to say farewell to the relationship. A rich relationship should enable you to take some journeys as a couple and others alone.

Don't become a robot

It's easy to fall into the trap of work, supper, TV, bed, work, supper, TV, bed. The more you do, the more you'll want to do and the dream list above can help you do just that! And as you push back your boundaries outside work, it will also become much easier to do just that in your working life. At the start of this book, you identified what success and happiness meant to you. Perhaps you identified things like a large bank account, exotic holidays, happy, healthy kids who stay off drugs and alcohol, giving something back to the community which really makes a difference, a particular status in the community or organisation.

You need to decide how important success is to you and in what capacity. Occasionally, you may tweak or transform your ideas of success and happiness or completely change them. But in the hustle, bustle and noise of life, take time out to dream and look into the present and future to ensure you're spending your life on activities and with people who are important to you. Get focused and create the life and success you want.

Looking forward

The goal posts of life are for your own positioning. Be clear about the things you want to change in your life and what you want out of it, and then take personal responsibility to make it happen. You may need to work around barriers and obstacles and take regulations and rules into account along the way, but the journey makes the end achievement all the more rewarding.

Your degree over, you have a chance to look back, contemplate, reflect and congratulate yourself; and to look forward, to plan and build your future. Pause to do this at regular intervals in your life and it will feature the activities and achievements which are important to you.

Finally, consider what really is important in life. Do any of these elements feature for you?

1   *Love* and be loved.
2   Be *passionate* about a cause.

3   *Wonder* at the beauty of the earth and nature's sheer power.
4   Feel at *peace*.
5   *Laugh* and see the funny side.
6   *Care* for those you know and those you don't.
7   Be *curious*: don't lose the habit of asking what, why, when, where, who, how.
8   *Learn* from those who've gone before you and who'll come after you.
9   Use your *creativity* and *imagination* to the full.
10 *Create* you own luck, success and happiness.

And remember:

Nobody ever said: 'I wish I'd spent more time at the office' on their deathbed.

Summary action points

> *Your life*
> *Your future*
> *Your choice*
> *Good luck!*

Further reading

Career related

AGCAS Briefings and Information Booklets series, available from your university careers service, include:

> *Education Sector*
> *Health Sector*
> *Science Sector*
> *Environmental, Food Chain and Rural*
> *Postgraduate Study and Research*
> *Vocational Course Surveys.*

Your careers service will have others on a wide variety of subjects of interest and relevance to graduates.

Astor, B. (2003) *What Can You Do With A Major in Biology?*, New York: John Wiley & Sons Ltd.

Brown, C. (2005) *Working in the Voluntary Sector*, Oxford: How To Books Ltd.

Camenson, B. (2003) *Great Jobs for Biology Majors*, London: McGraw-Hill Book Co.

Camenson, B. (2004) *Careers for Plant Lovers and Other Green Thumb Types*, London: McGraw-Hill Education – Europe.

Chandler, C.R. (2007) *The Chicago Guide to Landing a Job in Academic Biology*, Chicago, IL: University of Chicago Press.

Deere, J. (2002) *Careers in Global Horticulture*, Florence, KY: Delmar.

Heitzman, W.R. (2006) *Opportunities in Marine Science and Maritime Careers*, London: McGraw Hill Higher Education.

Kreeger, K. (1998) *Guide to Non-Traditional Careers in Science*, London: Taylor & Francis.

Rothwell, N. (2002) *Who Wants to be a Scientist?: Choosing Science as a Career*, Cambridge: Cambridge University Press.
Sheldon, S. and Brown, M.R. (2000) *Opportunities in Biotechnology Careers*, London: McGraw-Hill Education – Europe.
Winter, C. and Belikoff, K. (2004) *Opportunities in Biological Sciences*, London: McGraw-Hill Book Co.

General career

Barrett, J. and Williams, G. (2003) *Test Your Own Aptitude*, London: Kogan Page Ltd.
Lees, J. (2006) *How to Get a Job You'll Love*, London: McGraw-Hill Education – Europe.
Williams, N. (2004) *The Work We Were Born to Do*, London: Element Books Ltd.
The Writers and Artists Yearbook, London: A&C Black Publishers Ltd.

Further study

Dee, P. (2006) *Building a Successful Career in Scientific Research: A Guide for PhD Students and Postdocs*, Cambridge: Cambridge University Press.
Marshall, S. and Green, N. (2006) *Your PhD Companion*, Oxford: How To Books Ltd. A great selection of tips and advice to help you through your PhD.

Recruitment

See the website www.alec.co.uk for lots of formats and examples of CVs.
Bishop-Firth, R. (2002) *CVs for High Fliers*, Oxford: How To Books Ltd.
Bryon, M. (2005) *Graduate Psychometric Test Workbook*, London: Kogan Page Ltd.
Johnstone, J. (2005) *Pass that Interview: Your Systematic Guide to Coming Out On Top*, Oxford: How To Books Ltd.
Yate, M.J. (2002) *The Ultimate CV Book*, London: Kogan Page Ltd.
Yate, M.J. (2003) *The Ultimate Job Search Letters Page*, London: Kogan Page Ltd.
Yate, M.J. (2005) *Great Answers to Tough Interview Questions*, London: Kogan Page Ltd.

Moving up the career ladder

Bishop-Firth, R. (2006) *The Ultimate CV: Win Senior Managerial Positions with an Outstanding Resumé*, Oxford: How To Books Ltd.
Hughes, V. (2004) *Becoming a Director*, Oxford: How To Books Ltd.

Purkiss, J. and Edlmair, B (2005) *How To Be Headhunted*, Oxford: How To Books Ltd.

Shavick, A. (2005) *Management Level Psychometric and Assessment Tests*, Oxford: How To Books Ltd.

Working abroad

Carté, P. and Fox, C. (2004) *Bridging the Culture Gap: A Practical Guide to International Business Communication*, London: Kogan Page Ltd.

Doing Business With, an excellent series published by Kogan Page Ltd covering these countries: Bahrain, Croatia, Saudi Arabia, UAE, China, Jordon, Kazakhstan, Kuwait, Lybia, Serbia and Montenegro and the EU Accession States.

Going to Live In ... and *Living and Working in ...* two highly informative and practical series published by How To Books Ltd (Oxford), covering countries such as Spain, Australia, New Zealand, France, Italy and Greece.

Reuvid, J. (2005) *Working Abroad: The Complete Guide to Overseas Employment*, London: Kogan Page Ltd.

Vacation Work has a plethora of publications which give you ideas on how you can work your way around the world. Visit www.vacationwork. co.uk.

Own business

Bridge, R. (2006) *My Big Idea: 30 Successful Entrepreneurs Reveal How They Found Inspiration*, London: Kogan Page Ltd.

Finch, B. (2006) *How to Write a Business Plan*, London: Kogan Page Ltd.

Gray, D. (2004) *Start and Run a Profitable Consultancy Business*, London: Kogan Page Ltd.

Isaacs, B. (2004) *Work For Yourself and Reap the Rewards*, Oxford: How To Books Ltd.

Jolly, A. (2005) *From Idea to Profit*, London: Kogan Page Ltd.

Power, P. (2005) *The Kitchen Table Entrepreneur*, Oxford: How To Books Ltd. Turn that hobby into a profitable business!

Reuvid, J. (2006) *Start Up and Run Your Own Business*, London: Kogan Page Ltd.

Whiteley, J. (2003) *Going for Self-Employment*, Oxford: How To Books Ltd.

Gap year/time out

Worldwide Volnteering Organisation (2004) *Worldwide Volunteering*, Oxford: How To Books Ltd.

Career and life success

Brown, S. (2005) *Moving On Up*, London: Ebury Press.
Drummond, N. (2005) *The Spirit of Success*, London: Mobius Publishing.
Hill, N. and Pell, A.R. (1996) *Think and Grow Rich*, London: Ebury Press.
Robbins, A. (2005) *Awaken The Giant Within*, London: Simon and Schuster.
Tracy, B. (2003) *Crunch Point: The Secret of Succeeding When it Matters Most*, New York: Amacom.

Skilling yourself

Bradbury, A. (2006) *Successful Presentation Skills*, London: Kogan Page Ltd.
Claxton, G. and Lucas, B. (2004) *Be Creative*, London: BBC Books Ltd.
Covey, S. (2005) *The 7 Habits of Highly Effective People: Powerful Lessons in Personal Change*, London: Simon & Schuster UK Ltd.
Lilley, R. (2006) *Dealing with Difficult People*, London, Kogan Page Ltd.
Parsloe, E. (1999) *The Manager as Coach and Mentor*, London, CIPD.
Wiseman, Dr R. (2004) *The Scientific Story of the Lucky Mind*, London: Arrow Books Ltd.

Managing others

Charney, C. (2001) *Your Instant Adviser: The A–Z of Getting Ahead in the Workplace*, London: Kogan Page Ltd.
Morris, M.J. (2005) *The First-Time Manager*, London: Kogan Page Ltd.
Taylor, D. (2005) *The Naked Leader*, London: Bantam Books.
Whitmore, J. (2002) *Coaching for Performance*, London: Nicholas Brealey Publishing.

Building financial bases

Ahuja, A. (2006) *The First-Time Buyer's Guide*, Oxford: How To Books Ltd.
Bowley, G. (2005) *Making Your Own Will*, Oxford: How To Books Ltd.
Chesworth, N. (2004) *The Complete Guide to Buying and Renting Your First Home*, London: Kogan Page Ltd.
Palmer, T. (2006) *Getting Out of Debt and Staying Out*, Oxford: How To Books Ltd.

Life related

Fortgang, L.B. (2006) *Take Yourself to the Top*, London: Tarcher-Penguin.
Gaskell, C. (2005) *Transform Your Life – 10 Steps to Real Results*, London: Thorsons.

Useful addresses and further information

UK general

Association of Graduate Careers Advisory Services
Administration Office
Millennium House
30 Junction Road
Sheffield S11 8XB
Tel: 0114 251 5750
www.agcas.org.uk

Hobsons
www.hobsons.com
A website with lots of features to help you get that right job wherever you are.

Prospects
www.prospects.ac.uk
A huge source of information and useful links for graduates of every discipline.

UK regional (graduate) websites

Many of the websites below are designed to help graduates returning to the region or wishing to move to the area.
Yorkshire and Humber Region: www.graduatelink.com
Graduates Yorkshire: www.graduatesyorkshire.info
Graduates North East: www.graduates.northeast.ac.uk
Merseyside Business Bridge: www.business-bridge.org.uk
Merseyside: www.gieu.co.uk
Merseyside Workplace: www.merseyworkplace.com

North Midlands and Cheshire Employers Directory: www.soc.
staffs.ac.uk/eh1/emp2003.html
Staffordshire Graduate Link: www.staffsgradlink.co.uk
Graduate Advantage West Midlands: www.graduateadvantage.co.uk
Gradsouthwest.com: www.gradsouthwest.com
GradsEast: www.i10.org.uk
The Careers Group, University of London: www.careers.lon.ac.uk
Graduate Ireland: www.gradireland.com
Scotland Graduate Careers, managed by Services to Graduates
Group: www.graduatecareers-scotland.org
Scotland: Graduates for Growth: www.graduatesforgrowth.co.uk
GO Wales: www.gowales.co.uk

Work experience, internships and voluntary work

British Universities North America Club (BUNAC)
16 Bowling Green Lane
London EC1R 0QH
Tel: 0207 251 3472
www.bunac.org.uk

Council on International Educational Exchange
www.ciee.org
Offers long-term career-related placements or summer jobs in the
USA, teaching placements in Asia, adventure working holidays in
Australasia.

Do It!
www.do-it.org
Find out what opportunities there are to volunteer in the region
you live in.

Earthwatch
www.earthwatch.org
Opportunities for the scientist and non-scientist to make a
difference and contribute to research worldwide.

GO Wales
www.gowales.co.uk

Graduate Business Partnership
www.services.ex.ac.uk/businessprojects
Run by the University of Exeter.

Knowledge Transfer Partnership
www.ktponline.org.uk/graduates

Merseyside: Business Bridge
www.business-bridge.org.uk

National Council for Work Experience
Tel: 0845 601 5510
www.work-experience.com
enquiries@work-experience.org

Voluntary Service Overseas
317 Putney Bridge Road
London SW15 2PN
Tel: 020 8780 7200
www.vso.org.uk

West Midlands: Graduate Advantage
www.graduateadvantage.co.uk

Further study

Association of MBAs
25 Hosier Lane
London EC1A 9LQ
Tel: 0207 246 2686
www.mbaworld.com
Has a full list of accredited MBA courses, plus links to institutions, and details of the MBA fair, scholarships, awards loans. The Official MBA Handbook can be ordered from its website and gives you all the information you need to get started. There's also information about rankings.

British Council
10 Spring Gardens
London SW1A 2BN
Tel: 0207 930 8466
www.britishcouncil.org
The British Council has a network of offices throughout the UK and in 110 countries worldwide. Visit its website or one of its offices for more information on funding, scholarships and studying in the UK. The Council has a guide, UK Science, which describes how science and technology are organised in the UK.

Lifelong Learning
www.lifelonglearning.co.uk
Information on Career Development Loans for EU students which
is applicable to vocational courses only, plus Lifelong Learning
Partnerships.

National Union of Students
www.nusonline.co.uk

Ploteus
www.europa.eu.int/ploteus
The European Course search portal.

UK NARIC
Oriel House
Oriel Road
Cheltenham
Gloucestershire GL50 1XP
Tel: 0870 990 4088
www.naric.org.uk
The National Recognition Centre for the UK and National
Agency for the Department for Education and Skills. The only
official information provider on the comparability of international
qualifications from over 180 countries.

Postgraduate study and research

Find a Masters
www.findamasters.com

Find A PhD
www.FindAPhD.com
This website is the largest directory of PhD opportunities in the
UK.

**Higher Education and Research Opportunities in the United
Kingdom**
www.hero.ac.uk
An excellent section on research with links to the main research
councils, universities and others. Plus information on how to
disclose your findings as a new researcher.

National Post-Graduate Committee
www.npc.org.uk
The NCP represents the interests of postgraduate students in the UK. Information on funding, discussion boards, postgraduate facts and issues, and postgraduate careers.

New Route PhD
www.newroutephd.ac.uk

Postgrad Hobson
www.postgrad.hobsons.com

Prospects
www.prospects.ac.uk

Research

Research Councils
www.rcuk.ac.uk
The strategic partnership of the UK's seven Research Councils.

Biotechnology and Biological Sciences Research Council
Polaris House
North Star Avenue
Swindon SN2 1UH
Tel: 01793 413 200
www.bbsrc.ac.uk
The leading funding agency for academic research and training in the non-clinical life sciences in the UK. It also promotes international links.

Science and Technology Facilities Council
www.cclrc.ac.uk

European Science Foundation
www.esf.org

Intute
www.intute.ac.uk/healthandlifesciences
A huge resource for education and research.

Institute for Energy and Environmental Research
www.ieer.org

Medical Research Council
20 Park Crescent
London W1B 1AL
Tel: 0207 636 5422
www.mrc.ac.uk

Natural Environmental Research Council
www.nerc.ac.uk

National Endowment for Science, Technology and the Arts
www.nesta.org

**Community Research and Development Information Science
(CORDIS)**
www.cordis.lu/en/home.html
Information on European Union-funded research opportunities.

The Royal Society
6–9 Carlton House Terrace
London SW1Y 5AG
Tel: 0207 451 2500
www.royalsoc.ac.uk
An independent academy promoting natural sciences.

The United Kingdom Research Office (UKRO)
www.ukro.ac.uk
The leading information and advice service on EU funding for
research and higher education.

Universities UK
www.universitiesuk.ac.uk

The Wellcome Trust
Gibbs Building
215 Euston Road
London NW1 2BE
Tel: 0207 611 8888
www.wellcome.ac.uk
An independent charity funding research to improve human and
animal health.

Self-employment

British Franchise Association
Thames View
Newton Road
Henley-on-Thames
Oxon RH9 1HG
Tel: 01491 578 050
www.thebfa.org
For information on franchises, both in and outside the UK, finding a franchise, successful case studies and events, a list of members.

BusinessLink
www.businesslink.gov.uk
A network of business advice centres in England with allied bodies in Scotland, Wales and Northern Ireland, all accessible through this website.

Prime Initiative
Astral House
1268 London Road
London SW16 4ER
Tel: 0208 765 7833
www.primeinitiative.org.uk
Dedicated to helping those over 50 to set up their own business.

Prince's Trust
Tel: 0800 842 842
www.princes-trust.org.uk
Help for the 14–30 year old who wants to set up his or her own business or tackle barriers to employment.

Shell LiveWIRE
www.shell-livewire.org
Unlock your potential with this excellent website. Plus financial action planning and a fabulous business encyclopaedia. For 16–30 year olds who want to start and develop their own business.

Start-ups
www.startups.co.uk

Protecting your creativity

Institute of Trade Mark Attorneys
www.itma.org.uk

UK Intellectual Property Office
Concept House
Cardiff Road
Newport NP10 8QQ
Tel: 0845 9500 505
www.patent.gov.uk
For details on how to apply for registration, design, copyright and
trade marks. Its careers could be of interest, too!

Job websites

International

Get a Life
www.getalife.org.uk
Careers guidance and information for the public sector.

The Guardian
http://jobs.guardian.co.uk
Provides the latest news and links to recruitment websites with a
huge jobs section.

Reed
www.reed.co.uk
Lots of graduate vacancies online with plenty of good advice.

Talent for Europe
www.talent4europe.com
A website featuring jobs in all EU countries.

Workpermits.com
www.workpermit.com
Lots of information about immigration and visas worldwide.

Sector specific

Biofind
ww.biofind.com/jobs/
A database of oppositions and personnel available in the
biotechnology industry (US-based).

Bioscience at Work
www.biocareers.org.uk

Biotechnology Industry Organisation
www.biocareer.com
A website prepared by this, the world's largest professional organisation devoted to biotechnology and related disciplines.

The Biotechnology, Pharmaceutical, Life Science and Healthcare Portal
www.bioportfolio.com
Everything from a career centre to news, reports, drug discovery and more!

CSL Recruitment
www.cslrecruitment.com

Earthworks
www.earthworks-jobs.com/oceanogr.htm
Jobs in oceanography, marine biology, coastal science and more.

Ecsite UK
www.ecsite-uk.net
Represents science centres and discovery centres in the UK. Jobs are listed.

Environmental Opportunities
www.ecoemploy.com

Evolution Life Science
www.evolutionconsultants.com

Federation of American Societies for Experimental Biology (FASEB)
www.faseb.org
Focuses on jobs and careers in the life science, including job listings and careers resource centres.

Matchtech
www.matchtech.com
Matches permanent and temporary recruitment across a broad spectrum of organisations.

Monster
http://lifescience.monster.co.uk

Nature
www.naturejobs.com
Including job listings by region (including USA and UK), discipline, organisation and title, plus careers magazine.

New Scientist
www.newscientistjobs.com

OceanCareers.com
www.oceancareers.com
A US website with jobs, internships, profiles, professional societies and employment trends.

PhD jobs
www.phdjobs.com

ScienceAlert
www.sciencealert.com.au/life-science/index.php
Australia and New Zealand – jobs, news and more.

Science Jobs
www.sciencejobs.com

SRG
www.biologyjobs.co.uk

Jobs in universities, colleges and schools

ETeach
www.eteach.com

Higher education
www.jobs.ac.uk
The official recruitment website for staffing in higher education.

Times Educational Supplement
www.jobs.tes.co.uk
Lots of vacancies in education.

Government

Association of Public Health Observatories
Alcuin Research and Resource Centre
University of York
Heslington
York YO10 5DD

Tel: 01904 724 493
www.apho.org.uk

Council for Science and Technology
Bay 307
1 Victoria Street
London SW1H 0ET
Tel: 0207 215 6518
www2.cst.gov.uk

Department for the Environment, Food and Rural Affairs
Customer Contact Unit
Eastbury House
30–34 Albert Embankment
London SE1 7TL
Tel: 0845 933 5577
Outside the UK: +44 207 238 6951
www.defra.gov.uk

Department of Health
Richmond House
79 Whitehall
London SW1A 2NS
Tel: 0207 210 4850
www.dh.gov.uk

Environmental Agency
Rio House
Waterside Drive
Aztec West
Almondsbury
Bristol BS32 4UD
Tel: 08708 506 506 for general enquiries; there are also specific
hotlines for other topics, so check the website.
www.envionment-agency.gov.uk

Food Standards Agency
Aviation House
125 Kingsway
London WC2B 6NH
Switchboard: 0207 276 8000
www.food.gov.uk

Health and Safety Executive
Rose Court
2 Southwark Bridge
London SE1 9PH
Tel: 0845 345 0055
www.hse.gov.uk

Healthcare Commission
Finsbury Tower
103–105 Bunhill Row
London EC1Y 8TG
Tel: 0207 448 9200
www.healthcarecommission.org.uk/homepage.cfm

Health Protection Agency
7th Floor Holborn Gate
330 High Holborn
London WC1V 7PP
Tel: 0207 759 2700
www.hpa.org.uk/hpa/links/default.htm

Local government careers
www.LGcareers.com
Careers information.
www.LGjobs.com
Current job vacancies in councils.

Medicines and Healthcare Products Regulatory Agency
Information Centre
10-2 Market Towers
1 Nine Elms Lane
London SW8 5NQ
Tel: 0207 084 2000
www.mhra.gov.uk

The National Health Service
Tel: 0845 6060 655
www.nhscareers.nhs.uk

National Institute for Health and Clinical Excellence
MidCity Place
71 High Holborn
London WC1V 6NA
Tel: 0207 067 5800
www.nice.org.uk

Network UK – The Researchers' Mobility Portal

www.eracareers-uk.info

This is a resource for researchers who are planning to move to the UK, with lots of practical information about visas, language courses and more, plus the latest science research news on the website. This will also lead you to the European Researcher's Mobility Portals, over 30 in all.

Office of Science and Innovation

Department of Trade and Industry

1 Victoria Street

London SW1H 0ET

Tel: 0207 215 5000

www.dti.gov.uk/science

The Office is responsible for UK Science Policy and for funding basic research allocated through the Research Council. It maintains and develops excellence in UK science, engineering and technology.

Professional organisations and trade associations

The following are examples of professional and trade associations which relate to biological sciences. Many have international links with their peers abroad, so research their websites thoroughly. Some examples follow:

ANSInet Publications

www.ansijournals.com

Academic and scientific and biomedical journals in Asia.

Asia Pacific BioGRID Initiative

www.apbionet.org/grid

Asia Pacific International Molecular Biology Network

www.a-imbn.org

BioNetwork

www.investinbiotech.com

Provides industry stakeholders with information and knowledge on all aspects of the biotechnology industry.

European Public Health Association
EUPHA Office
Otterstraat 118–124
Postbox 1568
3500 BN Utrecht
The Netherlands
Tel: +31 30 272 9709
www.eupha.org

Euroscience
www.euroscience.org
A European association for the promotion of science and technology

US–ASEAN Business Council Inc., Health and Life Sciences Working Group
www.us-asean.org/life-sciences

The Institute of Public Health in Ireland
5th Floor
Bishop's Square
Redmond's Hill
Dublin 2
Ireland
Tel: +353 1 478 6300
www.publichealth.ie

World Health Organisation Headquarters
Avenue Appia 20
1211 Geneva 27
Switzerland
Tel: + 41 22 791 21 11
www.who.int
Visit www.who.int/about/en for access to regional offices contact information.

Professional bodies and societies

The following links are largely based in the UK. For listings outside the UK, check out www.scholarly-societies.org and enjoy its huge listings worldwide of scholarly societies. You can search by region or subject, including biology and environment, health and medicine.

Animal science

Institute for Animal Health
Compton Laboratory
Compton
Newbury
Berkshire RG20 7NN
Tel: 01635 578411
www.iah.bbsrc.ac.uk
There are also laboratories in Surrey and Edinburgh – check the
website for the most appropriate for you.

Bioinformatics

European Bioinformatics Institute
Wellcome Trust Genome Campus
Hinxton
Cambridge CB10 1SD
Tel: 01223 494 444
www.ebi.ac.uk

Biological engineering

Institute of Biological Engineering
www.ibeweb.org

Biology

American Institute of Biological Sciences
1444 I Street
NW Suite 200
Washington, DC 20005
USA
Tel: +1 202 628 1500
www.aibs.org
The AIBS has a brochure you can download from its website called
Careers In Biology.

Centre for Bioscience
Worsley Building
University of Leeds
Leeds LS2 9JT
Tel: 0113 343 3001
www.bioscience.heacademy.ac.uk

European Countries Biology Association
c/o Institute of Biology
9 Red Lion Court
London EC4A 3EF
Tel: 0207 936 5946
www.europeanbiologists.org

European Molecular Biology Laboratory
www.embl.org

Institute of Biology
9 Red Lion Court
London EC4A 3EF
Tel: 0207 936 5900
www.iob.org

The National Academies
www.nationalacademies.org
Advisers to the nation on science, engineering and medicines. Visit their career guides at http://nationalacademies.org/careerguides.html.

Biomedical sciences

Institute of Biomedical Science
12 Coldbath Square
London EC1R 5HL
Tel: 0207 713 0214
www.ibms.org

Biotechnology

Australia–New Zealand Biotech Alliance
www.biotechalliance.org

AusBiotech
www.ausbiotech.org
The body for the Australian biotechnology industry.

European Federation of Biotechnology
www.efb-central.org
Serves biotechnologists across Europe.

New Zealand's Biotech Industry Organisation
www.nzbio.org.nz

Botany and plant sciences

Botanical Society of America
www.botany.org/bsa/careers
Also has salary and job information.

Nature
www.nature.com/index.html
Science and medicine at your fingertips on your desk top –
journals, gateways, jobs, websties, regional, partners and more
from Nature Publishing Group.

UK-CHM, the UK Clearing House Mechanism for Biodiversity
www.chm.org.uk/default.asp

Conservation

Joint Nature Conservation Committee
Monkstone House
City Road
Peterborough PE1 1JY
Tel: 01733 562 626
www.jncc.gov.uk

World Conservation Union
www.iucn.org
The world's largest conservation network with some 10,000
scientists and experts.

Ecology

British Ecological Society
26 Blades Court
Putney
London SW15 2NU
Tel: 0208 871 9797
www.britishecologicalsociety.org

Ecological Society of America
www.esa.org/opportunities

Ecology.com
www.ecology.com
An ecological source of information.

Forensic science

The Forensic Science Service
Trident Court
2920 Solihull Parkway
Birmingham BD7 7YN
Tel: 0121 329 5200
www.forensic.gov.uk

Genetics

Human Genome Organisation
www.hugo-international.org

Healthcare management

Institute of Healthcare Management
18–21 Morley Street
London SE1 7QZ
Tel: 0207 620 1030
www.ihm.org.uk

Journalism/writing

Association of Author's Agents
www.agentsassoc.co.uk

Association of British Science Writers
Wellcome Wolfson Building
165 Queen's Gate
London SW7 5HD
Tel: 0870 770 3361
www.absw.org.uk

European Medical Writers Association
www.emwa.org

National Union of Journalists
Headland House
308–312 Gray's Inn Road
London WC1X 8DP
Tel: 0207 278 7916
www.nujtraining.org.uk

Science Media Centre
www.sciencemediacentre.org

Marine biology

IMarEST
Institute of Marine Engineering, Science and Technology
80 Coleman Street
London EC2R 5BJ
Tel: 0207 382 2600
www.imarest.org

Marine Science and Technology Portal
www.marinescienceandtechnology.com

National Oceanography Centre
www.soc.soton.ac.uk

Sea Grant Marine Careers
WHOI Sea Grant
193 Oyster Pond Road MS#2
Woods Hole
MA 02543-1525
USA
www.whoi.edu/science/marinecareers/index.php

Microbiology

American Society for Microbiology
www.asm.org

British Society for Immunology
Triangle House
Broomhill Road
London SW18 4HX
Tel: 0208 875 2400
http://immunology.org

British Society for Haematology
www.b-s-h.org.uk

http://hematolog.vinchi.ru/english/katalog/inetengl.htm
Useful links in haematology and oncology.

Society for General Microbiology
Marlborough House
Basingstoke Road
Spencers Wood
Reading RG7 1AG
Tel: 0118 998 1800
www.sgm.ac.uk

Virology Down Under
www.uq.edu.au/vdu/VDUlinks.htm

Pharmacology

Association of the British Pharmaceutical Industry
12 Whitehall
London SW1A 2DY
Tel: 0870 890 4333
www.abpi.org.uk

British Toxicology Society
Administration Office
PO Box 249
Macclesfield SK11 6FT
Tel: 01625 267 881
www.thebts.org

Medicines Australia
www.medicinesaustralia.com.au
Represents the research-based pharmaceutical companies in
Australia.

National Pharmaceutical Association
Mallinson House
38–42 St Peter's Street
St Albans
Herts AL1 3ND
Tel: 01727 832 161
www.npa.co.uk

The Pharmaceutical Society of Northern Ireland
73 University Street
Belfast BT7 1HL
Tel:028 9032 6927
www.psni.org.uk

Royal Pharmaceutical Society of Great Britain
1 Lambeth High Street
London SE1 7JN
Tel: 0207 735 9141
www.rpsgb.org.uk

Physiology

The American Physiological Society
9650 Rockville Pike
Bethesda
MD 20814-3991
USA
Tel: +1 301 634 7164
www.the-aps.org

The Physiological Society
PO Box 11319
London WC1X 8WQ
Tel: 0207 269 5710
www.physoc.org

Federation of Asian and Oceanian Physiological Societies
www.faops.org.my

Federation of European Physiological Sciences
www.feps.org

Institute for Neuro-Physiological Psychology
www.inpp.org.uk

International Union of Physiological Sciences
www.iups.org
It has an excellent list of worldwide members at www.iups.org/
Sections/memsoc.html

Recruitment and employment

Recruitment and Employment Confederation
15 Welbeck Street
London W1G 9XT
Tel: 0207 009 2100
www.rec.uk.com

Research

Institute of Clinical Research
Thames House
Mere Park
Dedmere Road
Marlow
Bucks SL7 1PB
Tel: 01628 899755
www.icr-global.org

International Federation of Pharmaceutical Manufacturers and Associations
www.ifpma.org

National Institute for Medical Research
The Ridgeway
Mill Hill

London, NW7 1AA, UK
Tel: 020 8959 3666
www.nimr.mrc.ac.uk

National Institutes of Health
9000 Rockville Pike
Bethesda
Maryland 20892
USA
Tel: +1 301 496 4000
www.nih.gov
The National Institutes form a part of the Department of Health
and Human Services in the USA and they are the primary agency
for conducting and supporting medical research.
Lists of institutes and centres can be found at www.nih.gov/icd

Teachers

Association for Science Education
College Lane
Hatfield
Herts AL10 9AA
Tel: 01707 283 000
www.ase.org.uk

Teaching and Development Agency for Schools
151 Buckingham Palace Road
London SW1W 9SZ
Tel: 0207 023 8001
www.tda.gov.uk
Visit www.fasttrackteaching.gov.uk if you want to be a leader in
education in England at primary, secondary or special schools.

University and College Union
www.ucu.org.uk

Women in science

Daphne Jackson Trust
Department of Physics
University of Surrey
Guildford
Surrey GU2 7XH
Tel: 01483 689 166
www.daphnejackson.org
Help with career breaks and returning to work in science and engineering.

UK Resource Centre for Women in Science, Engineering and Technology
Listerhills Park
40–42 Campus Road
Bradford BD7 1HR
Tel: 01274 436 485
www.setwomenresource.org.uk
Great role models, careers information, useful links and more!

WISE
Women in Science, Engineering and Construction
6th Floor
10 Maltravers Street
London WC2R 3ER
Tel: 0207 557 6479
www.wisecampaign.org.uk

Zoology

Association of Zoos and Aquariums
www.aza.org
Job listings.

Institute of Zoology
Zoological Society of London
Regents Park
London NW1 4RY
Tel: 0207 449 6610
www.zoo.cam.ac.uk

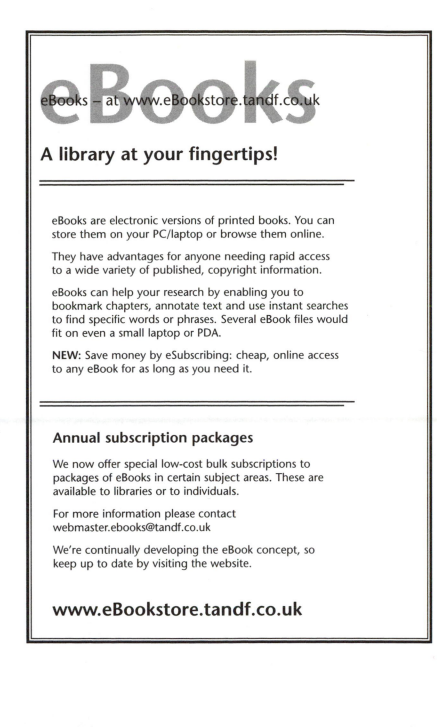